ANSWERS TO QUESTIONS THAT BUG BELIEVERS

Robert H. Mounce

BAKER BOOK HOUSE
Grand Rapids, Michigan

Contents

Foreword

One of the pleasant associations of my journalistic career was a working relationship with Bob Mounce, whom I hold in high esteem.

Questions of all sorts pour in over the transom of the editor's office at *Eternity* magazine every working day. They range in quality from the old chestnut, "Where did Cain get his wife?" to intelligent, penetrating queries that often enable Bob Mounce to turn out a good "Here's My Answer" column.

The questions cover a wide variety of subject matter dealing with Biblical interpretation and the practical, ethical aspects of the Christian walk.

Bob Mounce is able to field such a diversity of questions because he is one of those rare individuals who combines Biblical scholarship with warm insight into human problems. He knows the ways of the world and the message of the Word. Furthermore, he is able to express himself in down-to-earth, non-technical language.

Mounce is aware of the changing currents of thought but his rich understanding of Holy Scripture has provided him with deep spiritual perception. He is also devout without being stuffy.

I heartily commend this practical little book.

Russell T. Hitt
Former Editor,
Eternity magazine

Preface

I used to ask, Who do they think they are—these people who furnish answers to everybody's questions? How presumptuous! Then, quite by accident, I joined their ranks. Now, after meeting deadlines for more than seventeen years (the last ten with ETERNITY magazine), I am beginning to realize how fortunate my lot has been. Had it not been for your questions I probably would never have pursued all the interesting avenues of thought they brought to my attention.

Some of the questions have asked for factual data— and these have not been difficult to answer. A few good reference works will provide the answers to such queries as, What is the average rainfall at Beersheba? or, Which is the highest mountain in Palestine?

The vast majority of questions, however, have been of a different sort. They have called for interpretation and personal opinion. No Bible dictionary will discuss the question of gospel rock music or suggest how you might overcome periods of depression. Whenever a question involved the interpretation of a specific Biblical passage, I have drawn upon the exegetical work of Biblical scholars who hold Scripture in highest esteem. For questions where an opinion is all one can expect, I have tried to present my own best thoughts in a balanced and reasonable manner.

Every now and then someone asks, Do people really send in questions, or do you make them up? The answer to both parts of the query is, Yes. Readers *do* submit questions, and these are answered, if not in the column, then by personal mail. Other questions arise out of normal contacts in life. For instance, students pose questions which I judge to be of interest to a wider audience; conversations with people in churches and weekend retreats furnish a whole store of questions for future columns. Then—and here's my confession—every so often I make one up, just for the fun of it! After all, I have questions too—and the column is called "Here's My *Answer*," not "Here's My Answer to *Your* Question"!

Several years ago I took occasion to comment on my role as an "answer man." In the January, 1971 edition of *Eternity* I wrote:

> For about three and a half years I have been doing my best to answer the various questions you have sent my way. It's been great fun. Your questions have forced me into all sorts of interesting byways which otherwise might have been left unexplored. Looking back over my columns, I note that the vast majority of questions called for an interpretation or an opinion rather than what might be called hard factual data. Apparently, the problems that trouble us are not those whose solutions lie readymade in some answer book. We are primarily interested in learning what others think about those concerns for which there is no easy answer.
>
> In suggesting answers to your questions I have tried to stay as close to Scripture as possible. I accept the Bible without reservation as the Word of God. At times Scripture is absolutely clear and I have been able to say, "Thus saith the Lord." At other times it has been necessary to project an answer from the indirect evidence of Scripture. At all times I have tried to steer a course between theological demagoguery and that style of tolerance which, in its desire to slight no alternative, is forever moving away from any hope of positive statement.
>
> In the continuing attempt to develop a unified understanding of life and truth, I have not accepted some of the interpretations important to you, and I have espoused others which apparently are anathema to some. At times you have written to the editor to correct my ignorance. I am deeply appreciative of even the most minimal kind of dialogue. In a moment of candid humility Thomas Edison said, "We don't know the millionth part of one percent about anything," and I don't think the odds have changed appreciably since then.

Several months ago, while looking through the columns, I realized that they fell into two broad categories. One group might be called The Christian and Contemporary Society, and the other, The Bible and Its Interpretation. I also discovered that the majority of questions in the first group fell easily into one of seven smaller units. These, in turn, have become the seven chapters of the book. Since the material is arranged in a thematic sequence the finished work has a kind of direction to it. Some columns have been expanded with additional information and insights; others have been shortened or omitted. The question and answer format has been retained so the reader will be able to locate a specific question and its answer.

I am indebted to *Eternity* and its editors, Russ Hitt, Bill Petersen, and Stephen Board (who have always been genuinely supportive of my literary efforts), for permission to rework material which first appeared there into this form. I trust that reading the book will be as pleasant (and helpful) to you as writing it has been for me.

Robert H. Mounce

1

Facing Life's Problems

Jesus said, "In the world you have tribulation," but he did not end His statement there. He added, "but be of good cheer; I have overcome the world" (John 16:33). Most Christians are painfully aware of the first part of the verse. Life has a full measure of irritations, frustrations, and obstacles of every sort. That Jesus has overcome this world makes for good theology, but too seldom actually results in good cheer on the part of the believer. Chapter one is about "tribulations"—and how a practical faith in the overcoming Christ can result in "good cheer."

SHOULDN'T THE CHRISTIAN HAVE FEWER PROBLEMS IN LIFE THAN THE NON-CHRISTIAN?

The claim that "Christ is the answer" has sometimes been misunderstood to mean that those who are in Christ no longer have any problems. We may as well face it—to be alive is to have problems! In no sense is the

Christian immune from them. Whether he has more or fewer problems than the non-Christian is hard to say. In any case, they tend to be of a different sort. The non-Christian is troubled by those obstacles in life which keep him from fulfilling his goals. The Christian is troubled by his failures to allow the Christ-life to find expression through him. While the frustrations may arise in part from similar irritations the two orientations are distinctly different.

The Christian's real problem is not the problem itself but his attitude toward it. Some try to walk through life with their eyes closed to problems. They tell themselves that whatever they refuse to recognize doesn't exist. Others spend their time dreaming of a never-never land where all of life runs smoothly without a ripple of discontent. They assure themselves that if circumstances were only different they would live the full and happy life. This attitude is reducible to the startling proposition: if problems didn't exist, I would know how to meet them.

In the Book of James we find God's way to meet problems. He says in effect, "Accept life's problems with joy because every trial is part of the obstacle course whose finish line is Christian maturity and whose prize is spiritual stamina." This is the outlook of the hearty soul who exclaims, "Bring me problems; good news leaves me weak!" Here is zest for life in its fullest sense. Here is the spirit which flings itself with abandon into the game of life rather than retiring to the sidelines fearful of injury and overly concerned about the minor bruises of some past skirmish.

If there is anyone who should radiate the sheer joy of living—problems and all—it is the one who, having the Son, has life. David's last word to Solomon was, "Be strong, and show yourself a man" (I Kings 2:2).

Problems? Yes! But praise God for the wisdom to meet them (James 1:2-8) and the will to win through.

WHY DOES GOD ALLOW HEARTACHE TO ENTER THE LIVES OF HIS CHILDREN?

A rather definitive answer to this question has already been written. In my opinion the best treatment of the subject is found in C. S. Lewis' *The Problem of Pain* (Macmillan, 1948). Among many other insights, Lewis notes that "the full acting out of the self surrender to God, therefore, demands pain" (p. 87). Pain is a vital part of God's method of conforming believers to the image of His Son.

WHY CAN'T I STOP BEING IRRITABLE?

It is so easy in today's rapidly moving world to lose our composure. Little things get blown up out of all proportion. Everything rubs us the wrong way.

Irritability is the outward expression of inner frustration. We become frustrated when we are hindered from achieving our goals.

And this is precisely the point: Our goals are *ours* rather than God's. He is concerned with the process of character building that takes place within us, while we are concerned with what can be accomplished through us. How many of us can accept our limitations as part of God's gracious gift? We are often so neurotically anxious to *remake* life rather than simply *live* it in the glow of His presence.

Most irritability stems from our own selfish demands upon life. It witnesses to an inner frustration which rises from a refusal to accept in humility the lot in life assigned by God. "The chief end of man" says the

Westminster Shorter Catechism, "is to glorify God and enjoy Him forever." The road to inner serenity lies in this direction.

I AM CRITICAL OF SO MANY THINGS IN LIFE. IS THERE ANY WAY TO GET OVER THIS?

Apparently, negativism is a universal expression of man's basic insecurity. People seem to have a psychological need to project onto others what may be termed vicarious guilt.

In order to compensate for our own inadequacies, we force on others a standard so stern and uncompromising that their failure—which is inevitable—becomes, in some strange way, our vindication. To be sure, people fall short of ideals, both their own and those of society, but to make human fallibility an occasion for heightening our own stature is as neurotic as it is unrealistic.

Genuine compassion binds all men together in love. In the great human family there are no doctors and patients, but only invalids at various stages of recovery. We are not asked to increase each other's distress but to help one another toward health. Recovery begins with the personal realization that Christ died to save us, not so much from hell as from the malignant and distorting power of our own self-centeredness. To grasp fully that we are accepted and forgiven by God in and through Jesus Christ frees us from the frantic necessity of proving our superiority by tearing others down.

Criticism is the public announcement of one's own woeful lack of spiritual maturity. To love as Christ loved is to extend an acceptance which ignores the failings of others. May God grant us compassion and a sense of corporate responsibility for the conduct of all men and our fellow-believers in Christ in particular.

SOME DAYS I WAKE UP FEELING DEPRESSED AND I CAN'T SEEM TO SHAKE IT OFF DO YOU HAVE ANY SUGGESTIONS?

I must note that I have absolutely no professional knowledge of psychotherapy. I understand that depression may be organically caused, and in many cases it needs the attention of a clinical psychologist or a psychiatrist. However, if your depression is more like what we may call a "bad day" then some suggestions are in order.

I find that when I am down in the mouth it is almost impossible to decide to "cheer up" and then make it work. Either I can't or I don't want to. But there are two approaches to the problem on a practical level. One is to go to work and forget about it. I'm not sure a person can think himself out of despair. Inactivity seems to complicate the problem and deepen the frustration. Another approach is to realize that while you can't do much about it this time, you can try to understand what might have caused it, and avoid it next time around. For me, a series of late nights, too much work for a given period of time, and concern about things I can't change, all take the lilt out of living. The first I can take care of with a bit of forethought. The second is more often than not the result of procrastination. The third is sheer foolishness. Once you know what will cause a "bad day," steer around it! There is no virtue in fighting unnecessary battles and only the perverse delight in defeat.

I'VE BEEN TERRIBLY DISCOURAGED THE PAST FEW MONTHS BUT CAN'T FIGURE OUT WHY. WHAT CAN A CHRISTIAN DO ABOUT DISCOURAGEMENT?

Many situations in life can trigger discouragements. Yet seldom is one specific incident really responsible. More often than not people just get run-down physically. Contemporary society rushes headlong as if the only important thing were to get life over with. Inadequate rest, nutrition, and exercise—to say nothing of emotional strains affecting the body—all contribute to a physical condition in which resilience and confidence are next to impossible.

So part of the antidote to discouragement is to restore physical vitality. Let me warn you, this is harder than you think. It is not easy to add a jogging routine to an already hectic life. And not only must positive action be taken; detrimental activities—late nights, crisis living and tension-filled personal relationships—must be abandoned. The intricate relationship between the physical and the psychic is not fully understood but it is everywhere acknowledged that they affect each other to a far greater degree than was formerly believed.

Another source of discouragement is man's tendency to aspire beyond his ability to achieve. A modern beatitude might be, Blessed is the man content to live within the normal limitations of his God-given abilities. Phillips' rather striking translation is "Make it your ambition to have no ambition" (I Thess. 4:11).

It seems as if in every area of life we would like to move up just one step. One step *at a time*, that is. But unfortunately, this desire doesn't abate when we reach the threshold of our competency. The Peter principle (that in every bureaucracy people tend to advance until they reach the level of their incompetency) is relevant to discouragement. In our mad scramble "up" the ladder of success we are given to fits of discouragement whenever our hopes for self-advancement are frustrated. Then when we reach the limits of our ability (or have taken the last tragic advancement into a position for which we are not competent), we are doomed for continual disappointment because we still want to rise but the realities of life refuse to honor our childish expectations.

To put it simply, discouragement in many cases is the normal penalty for our unwillingness to live within the will of God as it relates to our specific role in life.

Moments of discouragement are a normal part of life. Of course it hurts when something you want doesn't materialize. Who enjoys a No to the sincere question, Will you marry me? Or who delights over a letter saying that the job you'd love has just been filled by someone else? No sense denying that these disappointments hurt. But they all go away. That is, they do if the individual has a healthy attitude towards life. Prolonged discouragement indicates not so much the debilitating force of the setback as it does the emotional, physical and (often) spiritual condition of the person himself.

For the believer honestly committed to the will of God for every aspect of his life, disappointments are but momentary periods of testing and strengthening. It requires no character to enjoy getting what you want. But God is not interested in hollow people or shallow experience. His purpose in the world requires maturity, resilience and determination.

TERRIBLE THOUGHTS KEEP RUNNING THROUGH MY MIND AND I CAN'T SEEM TO STOP THEM. CAN YOU HELP?

In a situation as severe as this question implies, I would suggest that you share your problem at length with a pastor or a Christian friend in whom you have real confidence. Because the problem of an uncontrolled imagination is fairly common, however, a few general comments are in order.

In Rev. 12:10 Satan is called "the accuser of our brethren." Although he is the "deceiver of the whole world" (v. 9), he has and can be conquered by the faithful on the basis of the redemptive work of Christ (v. 11).

One of the major activities of Satan is to rob believers of their joy and peace in Christ. Disguised as an "angel of light" (II Cor. 11:14), he finds all too easy access into the lives of Christians. James promises that if we resist the devil he will flee (4:7) and advises, "Draw near to God and he will draw near to you" (v. 8). I've never known this to fail.

John writes that when our hearts condemn us, we may take courage knowing that God, being greater than our hearts, can see beyond our mental and emotional state to the intentions and desires of our heart (I John 3:19-20). This should bring great comfort to the troubled soul.

"Bad thoughts" that flit through the mind cannot be controlled by sheer will power. Instead, concentrate on rejoicing in your complete forgiveness. Fill your life with acts of kindness and concern for others. Read Romans 8:31-39 daily, inserting your own name in the appropriate places. God is on our side! What more could we ask?

DO YOU EVER HAVE DOUBTS ABOUT GOD AND THE CHRISTIAN FAITH?

One of the problems which often causes serious soul searching on the part of young Christians is the problem of doubt. It seems wrong to doubt God, yet from time to time questions slip into our consciousness unawares.

It is unfortunate, but in the religious culture in which most of us find ourselves, any lapse of enthusiastic confidence is often interpreted as the first step toward

18

atheism. Hence we tend to avoid "dangerous" questions, stifle honest concern, and maintain confidence by striving for a "positive mental attitude."

However, doubt is an essential part of our finitude. In a real sense only He who is infinite possesses that perfect knowledge which removes every trace of uncertainty. Beyond that, doubt is a frailty that plagues human nature as a result of the original act of disobedience. Knowing ourselves to be capricious we project our weakness onto God.

Doubt, however, is not the same as unbelief. The one is a weakness, the other a settled habit of the will. The rejection of God's redemptive work in Christ Jesus is a decision *not* to believe. It requires man to ignore a considerable body of objective evidence, deny his inner yearnings for wholeness, and turn a deaf ear to the persuasive voice of the Holy Spirit. Doubt, on the other hand, is a temporary wave of uncertainty which affects even the most mature believer. It rises from our human nature, and it can be countered by faith. We were never intended to lie to ourselves about what we are by nature —the old man has not improved one whit since we came to Christ. But he is powerless before the presence of the indwelling Spirit and is quickly put to flight by honest confession.

Even John the Baptist, of whom Jesus said, "Among those born of women there has risen no one greater" (Matt. 11:11) had his doubts (see Matt. 11:3).

Doubt is the dark side of faith. It is our finiteness demanding knowledge in an area where only faith is appropriate. But doubt should neither be feared nor avoided. Named for what it is—an integral part of our humanness—it loses its threat. Like a shadow brought out into the light, it disappears.

IS COMPROMISE EVER RIGHT?

In discussions about ethics and morality, the word *compromise* has a rather sinister sound. The compromiser is pictured as one who is willing to act against his principles in order to achieve some immediate and selfish gain. Shifty eyes and a weak handshake! Because the word is surrounded by such unfavorable connotations, it will be well to establish some sort of basic working definition. Most dictionaries list as the primary meaning the idea of settling by mutual concession. A compromise is the process of arriving at a solution acceptable to each party.

A moment's reflection will indicate that compromise is the basic pattern of civilized conduct. If two people arrive simultaneously at a door, they both step back to allow the other to enter. If I call to your attention a piece of work which you have done for me which falls below my expectations, you point out the limitations which make perfection impossible and rework the project to the best of your ability. We have reached a compromise.

Part of the problem with the idea of compromise arises from the fact that we tend to view all principles as absolute and existing on a single level. It is confusing to realize that every situation of life brings into play a number of principles somewhat at odds with each other. It is even more confusing that these principles themselves must be ordered into a hierarchy of theological and ethical significance. But whether we recognize it or not, our choices reveal priorities and involve compromises. If you tell a lady sporting a ridiculous headpiece that you like her hat, you reveal that courtesy is a higher principle for you than honesty. Even if you don't say a word to the lady, you are communicating to her that you find nothing offensive about her hat—another untruth.

The important thing for the Christian is that his compromises conform to the pattern of revelation. The great commandment is to love God and one's fellow man. This is the ultimate principle which gives structure and priority to all human relations. It is the only principle which may never be compromised. It cannot make a single concession: it is never right not to love. In one sense, the Incarnation is the supreme compromise. God became man in Jesus Christ to redeem mankind from sin. This magnificent concession did not compromise love, but was an expression of the ethical primacy of that love. The church as the body of Christ desperately needs to learn the art of adjusting all its conduct to this ultimate principle.

HOW CAN YOU LOVE A PERSON YOU DON'T EVEN LIKE?

If I accept the principle that it is never right not to love, then the question poses an extremely practical problem.

The usual rationalization in response to the command, "Love one another" is to reinterpret the meaning of love. Some people redefine love as a willingness to be concerned about the welfare of others which does not necessarily involve any obligation to respond personally to the other as an individual. There is no other way, we are told, that we could obey the command. How can we love everyone when we obviously have little control over our personal likes and dislikes?

Somehow this approach just doesn't satisfy. Is God's love—and this is our model—only a decision to put up with us and save us even though He doesn't like us very much? Perhaps our emotional reaction against certain people is more a disclosure of our own unloveliness than that of the other person. Granted, we may disapprove of a man's conduct or attitude, but does this give us license to dislike the man himself?

If we see all men as those for whom Christ died as well as seeing what each can become by the transforming power of God, will we treat ourselves to the luxury of a deep and subtle sense of superiority? To do so is to take sides against Christ in His great and compassionate concern to redeem men from the power of sin and remake them in His own image.

IF WINNING IS SO IMPORTANT IN AMERICAN LIFE, HOW CAN WE BE EXPECTED TO LEARN TO LIVE WITH OUR FAILURES?

The idea of competition has long been a vital ingredient in the American recipe for success. It was the hearty and foolhardy who left the security of the old country for adventure and prosperity in the new world. Settlers moved west to find better land and better opportunities. The concept of frontiersmanship carried over into business and industry. "May the best man win" has historically been the most accurate slogan for the American way of life. From fingerpainting contests in kindergarten to playing in the Superbowl we have learned that winning is everything.

What this implies about losing is quite obvious. Losing is an open admission of failure. If winning is everything, then second place is worthless. Losers in the semifinals play what we patronizingly call the "consolation match." One reaction to this compulsive psychosis about being number one is the tendency among many of the younger generation to refuse to compete. They call for cooperation in place of competition—and who can deny the appeal of this more altruistic stance? Yet, we ponder, isn't the competitive market of free enterprise the secret of American economic success?

Is there any way we can preserve the value of winning without paying the devastating psychological price of failure? I believe there is. It lies in understanding the creative role of failure in personal growth. Here are some of the positive benefits of failure:

1. Failure helps us to accept a more realistic appraisal of our limitations. It is sheer fantasy to imagine that we can accomplish everything we want, given the right set of circumstances. Blessed is the man who doesn't require the warm glow of imaginary accomplishments! Yet not only children dream of knights in silver armor and beautiful maidens in prison towers. Adults need to realize that maturity, among other things, is the willingness to accept life's limitations good-naturedly. A new and rewarding era begins when the unrealistic expectations of youth give way to the more balanced perspective which grows out of the ego-shattering admission that, like the angels, we are still a little lower than God.

2. Failure is a major pedagogical device structured into human experience. Once success is a habit, what is there left to accomplish? Intelligent inquiry into failure has far more to teach than the comfortable acceptance of winning. And don't forget that when one fails, he is not necessarily a failure. Failure is a temporary obstacle in the path, but calling oneself a failure is abandoning the goal. In the simplest of terms, we learn by our mistakes.

3. A willingness to fail opens the door to all sorts of new and exciting possibilities in life. The greatest enemy of a life fully lived is the fear of failure. We tend to stay clear of anything in which we think we might not do well. The specter of public ridicule stifles the desire to try our hand at something new. The overly sensitive

withdraw into their shell of timidity rather than run the danger of looking bad before others. Hence, bookworms read more books, misers save more money, knitters knit more socks, and all that life could be passes them by. But what a glorious sense of freedom is enjoyed by those who are willing to fail! What tremendous exhilaration to discover that what others may think is not so important after all. As one wise person said a number of years ago, "You wouldn't worry so much about what others think of you if you realized how seldom they do!"

In all of this, I am not saying that failure should be a goal. However, failure is a normal part of life intended for our instruction and help. The same man who said, "I can do all things in him who strengthens me" (Phil. 4:13) also admitted that God's power is made perfect in human weakness (II Cor. 12:9). He came to this truth only after three failures to recognize the advantages of his thorn in the flesh.

Fear of failure seals the lips of countless Christians who would like to share their faith. In causing us to back off from difficult challenges, fear drains much of the zest from our life of faith. While faith in God does not eliminate failure, we know that in His infinite wisdom God allows that mixture of success and failure which will bring us as close as possible to what He wants us to be.

I HAVE A HARD TIME BELIEVING THAT GOD ACTUALLY WANTS PEOPLE TO BE "POOR IN SPIRIT." ISN'T IT TRUE THAT MOST IMPORTANT THINGS GET DONE BY MEN WHO ARE JUST THE OPPOSITE?

We must not interpret "poor in spirit" to mean poor-spirited. Jesus nowhere places a premium on timidity or discouragement. He does not say in Matt. 5:3 "Blessed are the doormats for theirs is the privilege of having everyone wipe his feet on them."

In the Old Testament the adjective "poor" is used to describe the helpless man who has put his entire trust in God. In such a state David confessed, "This poor man cried, and the Lord heard him" (Ps. 34:6). *Poor in spirit* is the opposite of all that is meant by the word *pride*. One who is poor in spirit recognizes his need for God, and does not consider his wonderful personality sufficient to make him a Christian. The God of infinite variety has made no two of us alike and yet we are all to be "poor in spirit," that is, totally dependent on Him.

The other thing that needs to be said is that we should not too quickly equate the work of God with "getting things done." One man may be a whiz at carrying through a building program; another may quietly and unassumingly teach his Sunday school class of five wiggly boys. Who is to say that the first is doing the more important job? Talents and gifts may vary but all are to be poor in spirit—the kind of people who acknowledge that it is God and God alone who is at work in and through what they are doing.

2

Developing
The Inner Life

The author of Proverbs admonished, "Keep your heart [the governing center of man's personal activities] with all vigilance; for from it flow the springs of life" (Prov. 4:23). Jesus taught that what lies at the core of a man will necessarily find expression: "For out of the abundance of the heart the mouth speaks" (Matt. 12:34). The inner life has always been of great concern to those who wish to establish and maintain an open and genuine relationship to God through Jesus Christ.

Yet it is at this very point where we most often fail. The outwardness of our faith can continue long after its inwardness has collapsed. Through the prophet Jeremiah, God promised that the day would come when He would put His law within the hearts of His people. He said He would "write it upon their hearts" (Jer. 31:33). Our greatest need is to nurture and develop this inner life. A. M. Hunter once wrote, "The secret of religion is religion in secret."

IN YOUR OPINION, WHAT IS THE QUALITY MOST LACKING AMONG CHRISTIAN PEOPLE TODAY?

The question places me in a negative stance which I don't particularly enjoy. Nevertheless, let me answer by suggesting several qualities which seem to me to be relatively scarce among Christians today.

First is a pervasive sense of joy. It is true that these are dreary days. We are confronted with wars, injustice, social anarchy, a rising drug culture, and overshadowing all else, the awesome possibility of a major atomic confrontation in which neither side can back down. Unfortunately, the Christian has become infected by his bleak environment. We reflect the pessimism of the world, and often forget that in Christ God has established an entirely new point of view. The love of God in giving His Son to die for our sins is a cause for optimism. To His despairing disciples Jesus said, "Cheer up! I've conquered the world" (John 16:33).

Another quality many of us lack is honest commitment. A person may be ideologically committed to a theological structure without being committed to the way of life which must necessarily grow out of it. Paul said that God "will render to every man *according to his deeds*" (Rom. 2:6). It is not the assertion of belief which proves salvation but the evidence of a transformed life.

Finally, I see a scarcity of Spirit-filled individuality. There is no need to argue that we live in an age of increasing conformity. Apparently, the last security available for American society is the security of being like others. In clothes, hair styles, attitudes, patterns of life, we are more and more alike. The pervasive influence of the mass media has subtly erased our differences, and Common Man with a Madison Avenue mindset is emerging. But the Christian is commanded by God not to "let the world squeeze you into its own mold" (Rom. 12:2, Phillips). This means that believers are to be nonconformists in an alien culture. Their nonconformity is not so much in the peripheral matters of dress and conduct, but a nonconformity of attitude—which results from an essential allegiance to the One who was crucified by the world. Jesus said, "If the world hates you, you know that it hated me first" (John 15:18). Our uneasiness with being different must be conquered, for it is axiomatic that every man of conviction must stand against his generation.

WHY DO SO MANY CHRISTIANS SEEM TO MAKE SUCH LITTLE SPIRITUAL PROGRESS IN LIFE?

Allow me to answer somewhat allegorically, with a discussion of tops and arrows.

The top is an interesting toy. Good tops that are well spun spin a long time in the same spot. Tops poorly spun wobble around in circles until they lose momentum and topple over. Neither kind, however, *goes* any place. They just *look* like they are making progress. Some tops even whistle to call attention to their spinning, but they too run down.

Many people are like tops. Some spin beautifully in one spot and others wobble erratically through life, bumping every obstacle within reach. Neither spinners nor bumpers, however, go any place. Both run down and come to rest about where they started.

An arrow, on the other hand, moves towards a goal. Everything about the arrow reflects its essential purpose. The straight shaft gives power. Carefully trimmed feathers guarantee a straight flight. The pointed tip insures penetration upon impact. The basic difference between an arrow and a top is that one is designed to move swiftly and accurately towards a goal while the other is made to spin, whistle, and amuse.

Some Christians are like arrows. They are goal-oriented. Their one consuming desire is to strike true at life's target. Everything about their lifestyle testifies to a purpose for living and a goal lying outside of themselves which is worth achieving.

Perhaps one reason why we spin and topple, whistle for attention and jostle one another in the process is that we have no clearly articulated goal in life. We have spun off into the whirling mass of other spinning tops and cannot steady ourselves long enough to ask where we should be headed. But tops are a childish and senseless activity which fails to move towards a meaningful goal. How much better to be an arrow: carefully drawn by the hands of reflective thought, aimed at the target of genuine spiritual obligation, hurled forth by the taut strength of the Master's will.

The future belongs to those whose purpose in life lies beyond the dizzy whirl of frantic activity. Tops belong to boys: arrows to men.

THE HARDER I TRY TO LIVE THE CHRISTIAN LIFE, THE MORE MISTAKES I SEEM TO MAKE. WHAT'S THE ANSWER?

I think that this difficulty—and it is common to a great number of Christians—stems from an inadequate understanding of what the Christian life really is. Christianity is not the satisfactory achievement of a certain level of performance, or a specific number of kindly acts and commendable attitudes. We are not called upon to satisfy some standard of conduct as a method of earning

God's favor. God is not an external examiner who sits above us taking careful notes of our failures.

The Christian life is essentially a life lived in conscious fellowship with God. He is on our side, not against us. Our relationship to Him is a family relationship. As His children, we draw upon His strength and wisdom as we live each day. Obviously, we fail—but in failing we are not sent away from home until we can guarantee our Father that we will never again make the same mistake. Like an earthly father, He is with us in our errors of judgment to help us learn and gain a new level of maturity.

One of the wonderful things about God is that He understands. I don't mean to say that He considers sin an unimportant and trivial matter. Sin put Christ, His Son, through the agonies of Calvary and for the first and only time brought separation into the eternal relationship of the triune God. What I do mean is that He knows the frailty of our human nature with all its tendency to wander. That's why He wants to stay right with us. Like a parent with a child who is just learning to walk, He is there to steady us when we lose our balance and start to fall.

But we so often leave Him behind. We begin our days with such confidence that we can go it on our own. At the close of day we realize that we've not been able to make it alone. But by then it is too late. So we ask His forgiveness, promise ourselves we'll work at it harder tomorrow, and go off to sleep with the uneasy feeling that there must be a better way.

And there is a better way. That better way is to take time each morning to remind ourselves that God wants to share the entire day with us. Unfortunately, many of us rush off to work without even thinking about Him.

He wants to go with us throughout the day, and enjoy with us all the good things that happen. In moments of disappointment He will speak a word of comfort. In the moment of decision He will gently impress upon our consciousness the right course of action. He will share our joys and lighten our sorrows.

If we approach the Christian life as an obstacle race or an endurance contest in which the only reasonable course of action is to try a little harder, we will never enter into the quiet joy of sharing our days with God. To those who labored under the heavy burdens of life, Jesus said, "Take my yoke upon you, and learn from me; for I am gentle and lowly in heart, and you will find rest for your souls. For my yoke is easy, and my burden is light" (Matt. 11:29-30).

Certainly, life has its problems. Just because I am a Christian doesn't mean that I am automatically sheltered from all the trials of life. What it does mean is that I have an eternal Friend who knows all about it and would like to help me through. What Christ says is, essentially, *Just calm down a bit; you can't do it by fighting so hard; why not back off and get the difficulty in perspective? Now, can you see that my way will save you from all sorts of unnecessary turmoil?*

The Christian life is exercising the confidence that God has the matter in hand. Our constant tendency is to take over and insist on providing enough worry and frustration so the whole world will know just how tough things really are. But faith rests in God's ability. That's what we need to do. Our trying harder is all too often the expression of our unwillingness to let God meet the need. Instead of struggling, how about trusting? Faith is not only the door to life, but also is its continuing principle of operation. Our task is to believe, not to assemble an impressive record of battles.

WHAT IS ACTUALLY MEANT BY THE EXPRESSION "SPIRITUAL LIFE?"

To many, "spiritual life" means something given to a person at salvation, nurtured by prayer and Bible study, and presented for entrance into heaven at the close of life. Those who define the phrase this way also usually consider man to be a "tripartite being," composed of body, soul, and spirit. Spiritual life is the resurrection of the human spirit (which is dead in sin and no longer functions as God-consciousness by the coming of God's Spirit.

It is interesting to note that while the word "spirit" occurs about six hundred times in the Bible (*ruah*, 378; *pneuma*, 220) the expression "spiritual life" is nowhere to be found. We read of spiritual gifts (I Cor. 14:1), spiritual songs (Col. 3:16), and spiritual sacrifices (I Peter 2:5) but not of spiritual life. This does not mean, of course, that the expression is without meaning, but it does explain why the phrase is unfamiliar to some.

What we do find in Scripture is the important fact that the life of the believer is not based on his own ethical striving. It is, rather, the outworking of an inward and supernatural transformation effected by the presence of God's Spirit.

It would be more correct to say that "spiritual life" is the life of the Spirit of God, resident in and controlling the life of the believer. Paul states it succinctly in Galatians 2:20, "It is no longer I who live, but Christ who lives in me." The *spiritual* life is His life. We are merely the instruments through whom He lives and labors.

This concept has the great value of destroying the basis for spiritual pride. We dare not boast of spiritual accomplishment because whatever has been achieved has been brought about by the presence of God's Spirit in our lives. Our responsibility is to remain open to Him and obedient to His prompting. And even then we are "unworthy servants: we have only done what was our duty" (Luke 17:10).

FOR YEARS I HAVE TRIED TO MAINTAIN A CONSISTENT AND REGULAR DEVOTIONAL PERIOD—AND FAILED. ANY SUGGESTIONS?

The devout and holy life has always been held up as an ideal. Ministers and conference speakers admonish hearers to be faithful in prayer and Bible study. Few, however, offer practical suggestions as to *how* this can be accomplished.

This problem is one that plagues the majority of Christians. The pace of twentieth-century life leaves scarcely enough time for what *must* be done to say nothing of what can be put off until another day. Unfortunately, we seem to think God can be put off indefinitely.

However, before we now indulge ourselves in the rite of self-deprecation (which is actually a paranoiac form of psychological self-atonement), let us examine more closely *why* we are so prone to wander. It is not because we lack time to do what is right. For we all know, deep down, that when all is said and done we do pretty much what we want to do. We also do not wander because we lack external stimuli to do right. Such reminders beat incessantly on our ears.

The root cause is the essential alienation of our souls from God. But, we may ask, wasn't that taken care of in salvation? Yes, in Christ we are reconciled to God, but salvation is not the wave of a magic wand which makes our old nature suddenly disappear. Instant perfection is not part of the bargain. Christians do not automatically home in on God. I have met very few believers who can hardly wait to get alone with God.

Before the picture gets too dark, however, let me also say that whenever we do draw near to God, He in turn draws near to us. And life is filled with moments when we desire Him more than all else. But normally these occasions do not come automatically. They are a result of an act of faith on our part. He stands outside the door and the invitation to enter must come from us (Rev. 3:21).

To realize this antipathy—the lingering result of an old nature that doesn't want to die—is the first step toward recovery. The second is to determine to place ourselves consistently in the sunlight of His presence. There is no other cure for the malignancy of human nature. The radiant glow of spiritual health is reserved for those determined to take the cure.

WHY IS IT SO DIFFICULT TO MAINTAIN A CONSISTENT PRAYER LIFE?

The answer is theological and quite simple: the "old man" in us doesn't want to pray. When we became united to Christ by faith, our old nature wasn't re-formed; rather, we became partakers of the divine nature (II Peter 1:4). Our desire to pray is this new nature seeking communion with its eternal source. But the old nature is still with us and not until Christ returns and we see Him as He is shall we be completely transformed into His image (I John 3:2). Only then shall we escape the harassment of an old nature which, although defeated by the cross, continues to dog our steps. Paul states the conflict in this way, "For the desires of the flesh are against the Spirit, and the desires of the Spirit are against the flesh; for these are opposed to each other, to prevent you from doing what you would" (Gal. 5:17).

34

Looking at the same problem from a slightly different perspective, I am inclined to think that our prayer life has a way of dwindling off because it isn't really a satisfying experience. As we tell our children, a person normally does what he wants to do most. If prayer is not personally rewarding it will gradually fade away like any other nonproductive option.

One reason why prayer may be less than satisfying is that we tend to think of it as a hands-folded-eyes-shut affair. But where in Scripture does it say that we should close our eyes when we pray? The usual rejoinder is that closing the eyes shuts out the distractions of the world. However, it also induces drowsiness or releases the imagination (which is infinitely more active without visual referents) to roam at will. Another byproduct of eyes-closed praying is a sepulchral tone of voice more suited to telling ghost stories than speaking with God. As Seneca, the Stoic philosopher, wisely said, "So live with men as if God saw you; so speak with God as if men heard you."

The more normal and conversational prayer becomes, the more satisfying the experience. The more satisfying the experience, the more often we pray. This does not mean that there will not be times of "groanings which cannot be uttered" (Rom. 8:26). But it does suggest that these times of deep heart searching will be supplemented with innumerable occasions of wide-awake dialogue with the resurrected, ever-present Lord.

I FEEL GUILTY ABOUT NOT BEING ABLE TO MAINTAIN A REGULAR DEVOTIONAL TIME. WHAT DO YOU SUGGEST?

First of all, cheer up a bit! This problem is by no means peculiar to you. I'm still looking for the first Christian whose "daily devotions" are all that he would like them to be.

One of the consequences of failing to live up to an ideal is a sense of guilt. The higher the standard, the greater the sense of failure. While there is no doubt that objective guilt exists, too often our discomfort is psychological guilt. Objective guilt has been taken care of by the death and resurrection of Christ. If we ask His forgiveness, it is given without reserve. But, we often continue to feel guilty. Apparently it is difficult to forgive oneself.

It seems to me that part of the problem lies in the idea that every morning we are to stop at a spiritual filling station to get sufficient fuel for the day's run through the arid regions of secularity. This monastic withdrawal and isolation views being "in the world . . . [but] . . . not of the world" (John 17:11, 16) in the physical sense only.

Let's put aside for the moment all our preconceived ideas of the spiritual life. What is it that the man Jesus wants from us? He wants to share in all that we do. He is not a spiritual consultant who passively waits in the prayer-closet for our arrival each morning, but a friend full of zest for life. He eagerly desires that we become close to Him and consequently become all that He intends us to be.

Make all your life a "regular devotional time." Meet Him in His Word—certainly. But never leave Him there! We live in a hostile world, but the believer can meet it head on. He has the buoyant expectation of one who knows that life at its center is a gift of God, grasped by faith, but carried through by constant companionship with the man Jesus.

WHY SHOULD I PRAY, SINCE GOD ALREADY KNOWS MY NEEDS AND HAS PROMISED TO SUPPLY THEM (PHIL. 4:19)?

It is perfectly true that we do not pray in order to let God know our needs. As the Omniscient One He possesses full knowledge of everything which pertains to us. There is nothing we can tell Him that He does not already know. Yet this same God urges us to bring all things to Him in prayer. Why? Part of the answer lies in the fact that God has somehow interwoven the prayers of His saints and what we might call the on-going redemptive history of mankind. In the same way that God has "limited" His sovereignty by giving man the awesome privilege of refusing salvation, so He has restricted His redemptive activity to the prayers of His children. "Prayer changes things" is more than a fond but unfounded hope. Activity which brings glory to God is at the command of the humblest believer. By prayer we allow God entrance to the area of our needs (of which He is already aware) to bless us with His presence and to supply us "according to his riches in glory in Christ Jesus."

While this interpretation stems from a wider understanding of the nature and activity of God as revealed in all of Scripture rather than from isolated proof texts, several verses are very much to the point.

James 4:3 says that we "have not because [we] ask not." Apparently our asking is necessary to our receiving. When Jesus returned to Nazareth, the townspeople were offended by the astonishing wisdom of the carpenter's son and "he did not do many mighty works there, because of their unbelief" (Matt. 13:58). So we see that unbelief can prevent the activity of God. II Peter 3:9 teaches us that it is not God's desire that any should perish—yet many do. If God could prevent this, but didn't, He would not be the God revealed in Scripture. We conclude that in His sovereignty, God has given man the right to refuse Him.

Prayer is the invitation to God to release His saving power in a given situation. He is not an overbearing supervisor who barges in to do Himself what He has given us to do. God's redemptive activity is not something forced upon an unwilling church but is inseparably interwoven with the prayers of His children.

IS THE PRAYER OF FAITH ALWAYS ANSWERED?

I assume that "the prayer of faith" means any prayer offered in confidence that God will answer. Matthew 21:22 is a verse often used to support this point of view: "Whatever you ask in prayer, believe that you will receive it and you will." Some feel that whatever they can somehow make themselves believe, will come to pass. God's answer to their prayer depends upon their subjective certainty. This kind of prayer has become the religious equivalent of the power of positive thinking.

Prayer is not designed for the confident, however, but for people in need. And overwhelming confidence is incompatible with a deep sense of inadequacy. The distraught father of the epileptic boy cried out, "I believe; help my unbelief!" (Mark 9:24). And Jesus answered his plea by exorcizing the unclean spirit. The man had faith but at the same time was racked with the torment of doubt.

Every verse in Scripture must be interpreted in the light of the entire Scripture. A single verse usually provides just one perspective on a subject which itself is much larger and needs to be understood as a whole. Other verses may qualify what appears to be the implication of a single verse. Obviously, "whatever you ask in prayer" cannot include anything contrary to the will of God revealed elsewhere in Scripture. Faith, therefore, is a requisite of answered prayer; but so also are such considerations as the worthwhileness of that which is requested, the appropriateness of an immediate answer to the spiritual growth of the suppliant, and the will of God as it relates to the specific request. It must be measured as a strand in the larger web of God's dealings with man.

WHY IS IT SO DIFFICULT TO DISCERN THE WILL OF GOD IN THE PRACTICAL DECISIONS OF LIFE?

I have found that college students and young married couples are especially puzzled about how to discover what the will of God is for their lives.

To be perfectly honest, and at the risk of being labeled theologically naive, I must say that I do not find it difficult to discern the will of God in most decisions which do come my way. It seems to me that when we are well acquainted with a person who is not capricous in his acts, it is not difficult to guess how he will respond to a given situation.

Since with God "there is no variation or shadow due to change" (James 1:17)—or as the *Twentieth Century New Testament* has it, "who is himself never subject to change"—He can be expected to act in a predictable manner. In fact, Paul prays that the Colossians may be "filled with the knowledge of his will" (Col. 1:9), a rather strange request if God withholds from His children what He wants them to do.

There is, in our day, a popular conception that God resists man's attempts to figure Him out. God is pictured as wrapping Himself in a cloak of secrecy in order to restrict man's knowledge. Eugenia Price's book, *No Pat Answers*, falls somewhat within this category. The author is intent on pointing out that in circumstances of life such as disappointments, failure, suffering and death, pat answers lead to confusion and bondage. In an introductory section entitled "What to Expect," she writes what is really a summary statement, "Freed of any attempt to explain God . . . I remain free."

Of course, there is no question whatsoever about the worthlessness of pat answers. A pat answer is by definition *too suitable*, hence, *contrived*. It does not follow, however, that all concise answers are therefore, "pat." When a lawyer asked Jesus, "Which is the great commandment in the law"—a tremendously complex question from the standpoint of Pharisaic thought—Christ answered, "You shall love the Lord your God with all your heart, and with all your soul, and with all your mind" (Matt. 22:36-37). The assumption that straightforward and relatively uncomplicated answers are necessarily "pat" answers is in itself a pat answer!

God is very much in the business of helping His children live each day as it comes along. His promise, "I will instruct you and teach you the way you should go" (Ps. 32:8) has not been canceled because a few uninstructed people think they know why children die or grownups get arthritis. God *does* make Himself known—He revealed Himself by sending His Son. The one who is "in the bosom of the Father"—that is, in the intimate presence of the Father, or "nearest to the Father's heart" *(NEB)*—"he has made him known" (John 1:18). The verb is *eksēgēsato*, from which we derive our word exegesis. Leon Morris says that this "indicates that Jesus has now given a full account of the Father" *(Commentary on the Gospel of John)*. Obviously, it does not mean that the nature of God is exhausted by His self-revelation in the Son. It does mean, though, that all we need to know to live the life He desires has been disclosed in Christ. This includes how to cope with life's obstacles such as disappointment, suffering, and doubt.

John 15:15 is an instructive verse on this subject: "No longer do I call you servants, for the servant does not know what his master is doing; but I have called you friends, for all that I have heard from my Father I have made known unto you." Friends of God are here described as those who obey Him. Apparently obedience is the key to understanding. Although the individual believer must apply the principles of divine action to particular cases, it is hardly right to suggest that the antidote for pat answers is to be "freed of any attempt to explain God." Jesus specifically told His disciples that if they continued in His word, they would know the truth and the truth would make them free (John 8:31-32).

WHICH DEVOTIONAL BOOKS HAVE BEEN OF GREATEST HELP TO YOU?

Daily fellowship in prayer and thinking on Scriptural truth can foster a satisfying relationship to Christ. Books and articles written by persons who have shared their lives with the Lord over a long period of time can also be helpful. Many Christians treasure some special book which, next to the Bible, has made a major impact on their lives.

A book that has affected me deeply is an anthology of devotional literature edited by James Mudge, titled *Honey from Many Hives.* God sent this book along at the very time I was experiencing something of a spiritual crisis and the unique way in which it spoke to my need made a lasting impression.

Of the many devotional books available today three others stand out as particularly helpful. The first is James Stalker's *The Trial and Death of Jesus Christ*. Stalker's remarkable insight into the inner life of the disciples and his sensitive portrayal of Calvary represent a high point in empathic literature. A second is J. Oswald Sanders' *Christ Incomparable*. In thirty-six concise chapters he has given us a compact and inspiring study of the person and work of Jesus Christ. While written for the "untaught in theology" it is by no means superficial. A book rapidly becoming a classic is John Baillies' *A Diary of Private Prayer*. Designed as an aid for morning and evening devotions it reveals the inner longings and aspirations of a man whose heart was supremely devoted to Christ. In it is found an exalted view of God, a breadth of concern for man, a refreshing regard for the commonplace, and an inspiring simplicity of faith.

The Christian Family

If Alvin Toffler's predictions are right (see his chapter on "The Fractured Family" in *Future Shock*) the American family faces a highly uncertain future. Most concerned parents are increasingly aware of the rapid erosion taking place in what has traditionally been the basic societal unit of western civilization—the family.

Christians may not opt for homosexual marriage, polygamy, or communalism, but they are beginning to feel the effect of a society which accepts temporary marriage as a standard feature. The widely-known family sociologist Jessie Bernard has said, "Plural marriage is more extensive in our society today than it is in societies that permit polygamy—the chief difference being that we have institutionalized plural marriage serially . . . rather than contemporaneously."

In the next few pages I would like to answer a number of questions which relate to the Christian family. Admittedly, the answers will be primarily opinion. However, I will try always to speak from a Biblical perspective; though in the complexities of life it is difficult to know how "Scriptural" one's opinions may be.

A major task of the modern theologian is to transfer the truths of divine revelation from their ancient setting in Biblical times to the contemporary world. In the process, there is no way to evade the arduous labor of careful historical analysis, balanced systematization, and intelligent reapplication. Historian Jacob Burckhardt's remark that "the essence of tyranny is the denial of complexity" is especially true in this context. Since every person is unique, there are no analogies in the realm of interpersonal relations which do not require additional comment.

DO YOU HAVE SOME HELPFUL SUGGESTIONS FOR RAISING CHILDREN IN THESE TROUBLED DAYS?

This question makes me smile a bit because here I am, your next door neighbor, being called upon to play the role of an expert in family counseling. An adequate answer would require more space and more wisdom than I have. Let me share a few thoughts, however, that may be of help. My remarks are directed to the parents of teenagers because, whatever the earlier roots of a problem may be, the problem itself seems to break out in the most disquieting way during the years of adolescence.

First, it is important to realize that children tend to become like the image they have of themselves. "Praise creates the condition desired" one wise mother has said. A healthy self-image will draw a level of conduct from a child that no amount of scolding will ever achieve. Constantly berate a child and he will begin to act like your opinion of him. Encourage him and support his positive qualities and he will try hard to be what you think he is.

Second, remember that young people are, by definition, young. If they didn't lack experience they could no longer be classified as youth. Their opinions and conduct necessarily spring from a limited exposure to life. Parental correction too often takes the form of censure instead of instruction. Remember that what they do makes pretty good sense to them. The wisdom which comes (or should come) from more extensive experience in living is simply not yet available. How could it be? In other words, don't expect children to act like adults. An old young person would be an abnormality. Life is a growing experience and is in no sense aided by unrealistic expectations.

We must remember that correction and guidance are not only necessary but perfectly normal in parent-child relationships. Besides, even at forty *we* don't act with perfect wisdom. Errors in judgment are opportunities for instruction. A succession of minor crises is intended for *our* development as well.

Next, understand that many of the more important things you teach your children are communicated without a single word on your part. We tend to be so exacting in those areas of child training which yield to ready evaluation ("Make your bed! Get off the telephone! Pick up your clothes! Be in at midnight!") and overlook the strategic importance of attitudes which are taught nonverbally—by the way we live. How many teenage accidents could be traced to a father's silent disobedience of posted speed limits? How often does bitterness or resentment in a young person simply reflect the atmosphere of tension and distrust created by parents unsure of themselves and their relationship to their children?

This is not advice to opt for silence, but only to remind that every day in a thousand ways we are teaching those under us by our actions and attitudes. Fortunately, children do not demand perfection. To watch Mother or Dad ask forgiveness or make right a wrong does not destroy their confidence in parents. Rather it teaches them how to go about accepting responsibility for their misdeeds.

Character is not the result of memorizing ethical dogmas but of being motivated to emulate available models. One of the most helpful insights I have received in a long time came from John M. Drescher's intriguing article, "Why I Stopped Praying for My Family" *(Eternity,* June 1971). The gist of the article was that Mr. Drescher stopped praying solicitous prayers for his family when he realized that if his children were to learn true love, then he as father would have to make visible the love of Christ in all his relationships with them and others. This is exactly what I am saying. In the moral growth of our children what we are far overshadows what we say.

Fourth, trust God and rejoice. Strange how easy it is to trust God for salvation and how difficult it is to trust Him in the details of living. He may not automatically transform a difficult child into a teenage saint, but He will grant parents wisdom, tact, and the power of the Holy Spirit as they seek for a clearer understanding of the problem and its answer. God knew what He was doing when He gave us each of our children. We might even say that since He got us into the situation He must also (as we do our part) get us out. Children are by nature happiness-oriented. They are far more susceptible to moral development in an atmosphere of cheerful acceptance than in the grim halls of mirthless correction.

DO YOU THINK THERE OUGHT TO BE ANY SORT OF GENERATION GAP IN CHRISTIAN FAMILIES?

The rapidly shifting value structure of contemporary society has placed severe stress on relationships between young and old. The young have suddenly found themselves with new advantages and opportunities while the old (in this case, over thirty!) are made to feel like members of the over-the-hill gang. Is this new division based on age something that belongs only in the secular world?

I am tempted to answer "No" and move on but that would be taking the question in a way I'm sure it wasn't intended. In one sense there is a gap that ought to exist between the generations—a gap that encourages young people to enjoy their youth thoroughly and enthusiastically and reminds adults to act their age. Worshiping at the fountain of youth (as if a doll face and a full head of hair were some sort of ultimate achievement) reveals a value structure that needs adjustment.

Educator (and senator) S. I. Hayakawa observed that what is commonly called a generation gap is more specifically a communications gap. Young and old live in increasingly different worlds. This is a fact of contemporary life. The psychological impact of a world caught in the throes of unprecedented change has shattered many existing structures in society and created new ones. The young, who are often psychological captives in an unreal world created by mass media, find it more and more difficult to talk with parents—who are short-tempered as they find themselves caught in the trap of their own technological achievements.

In the Christian home there is no real reason why a communications gap need develop. Parents do not have to allow the alien ideologies of Hollywood and Madison

Avenue to be uncritically accepted in the family circle. They should be aware of all the secular heresies which subtly teach that there can be complete personal fulfillment apart from the redemptive work and presence of Jesus Christ. Since dialogue is the order of the day, the Christian parent should be careful not to alienate his children by being overly authoritarian. Firm in his convictions and knowledgeable about the world in which he and his children live, he will do his prayerful best to demonstrate the persuasive logic of the teachings of Jesus.

At times I wish that someone could lay down ten simple rules which, if followed to the letter, would inevitably result in complete family tranquility—but it just doesn't work that way. Life is an art form in a constant state of change. God would move us out from the sheltered enclaves of imaginary utopias and into the mainstream of life itself. He wants us to find out for ourselves that His grace is sufficient and that the prizes of life are won by those in the race, not by those in the grandstand.

In considering questions which deal with the immediate problems of life, one discovers anew how interrelated are the difficulties of a person's life. It is virtually impossible to suggest a course of action which will serve equally well a number of individuals experiencing the same problem.

The less severe problems of life always seem to stem from some deeper dislocation, and this in turn supports the theological axiom that man in his natural state has turned his God-given capacity to love inward upon himself; and this basic perversion has set up a disharmony that runs throughout his entire being. It also permeates the society of which he is a part.

Answers to surface problems are helpful only so long as one realizes that they are at best finger-in-the-dike techniques and that the essential need of everyone is spiritual renovation. This begins with our justification, continues in sanctification, and issues ultimately with glorification. Perhaps an undue emphasis on salvation as conversion instead of progressive deliverance has dulled our understanding of God's intention for our growth in grace.

The problems of living together in constructive harmony all stem from the deeper problem of an unregenerate nature which lingers on like an unwelcomed guest. While we need all the help we can get now, there will be no complete deliverance until the inward change that began at conversion is carried through to completion and we are transformed to be like Christ (I John 3:2).

HOW IS IT POSSIBLE TO HAVE SUCCESSFUL FAMILY DEVOTIONS IN THIS FRANTIC WORLD IN WHICH WE LIVE?

I am quite sure that the question of family devotions troubles the conscience of Christian parents more than almost anything else. Devout parents, drawing heavily upon the devotional writings of former years, see a strong link between the disciplined and contemplative life and spiritual growth. The picture that comes to mind is that of the great saint of yesteryear rising before dawn for a lengthy uninterrupted period of prayer and insisting that the family go without breakfast rather than miss morning devotions.

Not for a moment would I speak disparagingly of Christian conviction so resolutely maintained. We profit greatly from those great saints' prodigious literary accomplishments (not to mention the uplifting influence of their piety).

Several observations, however, need to be made. The world in which these men lived moved at a much slower pace. The technological achievement of instant transportation did not tempt them with endless and seemingly urgent evening sorties. The Pied Piper of televised entertainment did not lure them away from active participation in constructive reading to the never-never land of passive tube watching. Apparently they went to bed at night. Few men arise regularly at four in the morning who drop into bed each night around midnight!

The world today not only moves faster and offers more action (and distraction), it is also much more fractured. The structures of authority have fallen or are in a state of serious disrepair. The institutions of society continue to display their badges, but no one seems to be paying much attention to them. A spirit of restless alienation permeates the American scene. With the decline of the family comes the cessation of all family functions. Once a center for growth and maturation, the home has become a launching pad for orbital flights into the new worlds of life outside. "Lost in Space" might well be written over what was once the normal home. In its simplest form, the question is, "How can people who rarely eat together ever manage to pray together?"

One answer to the problem would be to turn back the clock. We might find out that "things never were as good as they were!" In a recent *Time* essay on "The Meaning of Nostalgia," Gerald Clarke observed that "at a certain distance, vision fades and imagination takes over. . . . Nostalgia selects only what is agreeable, and even that it distorts or turns into myth." Not every Christian of last century arose before dawn to pray. And even those who did, in spite of their determination of purpose, experienced defeat at times. It was the apostle Paul himself who confessed that instead of doing the good he desired he found himself doing the evil he hated (Rom. 7:15, 19). Ideals are both necessary and right, but to punish oneself for failing in instant perfection is more masochistic than helpful.

Neither is it much of an answer to give it all up. There is a tremendous value in corporate family worship. Even when it doesn't work out as well as we had hoped, it is still a symbolic way of saying to our children that God is of sufficient importance to merit a segment of our family time each day. Those things are most real which we think about most. Certainly it is not in the best interests of our children to allow God to fade from the family circle by a sort of conspiracy of silence.

It seems to me that the answer in regard to family devotions lies along the following lines:

1. Make sure as parents that we sincerely want to spend time as a family with the Lord. Usually we manage to do what we want. It is amazing how few of our inherited values we have actually made our own. As members of the Christian subculture, we accept its mores with very little thought and seldom get around to thinking them through for ourselves.

2. Adjust to the fact that we live in the most rapidly changing era of history whose only sure prospect for the future is an increase in tempo. Family worship need not be at the mercy of the times, but neither can we ignore the realities of contemporary life. It is important that our worship belong to the twentieth century. If the attention span of modern youth is substantially less than that of an earlier generation, it is no answer to adhere doggedly to old drawn-out patterns. Such an approach alienates instead of creating the unity which we desire.

3. Make use of all the modern resources. The plethora of contemporary translations presents a wide selection of readable texts. The *wast* and *wert* of earlier days have given way to the more intelligible phraseology of today's translations. "Hey, I can understand *this!*" is heard with increasing frequency from our children.

4. Vary your approach. Kids like to read. Discussion will come if you don't squelch it. Don't hurry. Make it enjoyable. Try conversational prayer: it's much easier for youngsters, and it creates the feeling that Christ is really there—which, of course, He is.

Is it actually possible in the twentieth century for an average Christian family to read and pray together with any regularity? It is. Approach family devotions as a challenge. And don't give up!

SHOULD CHRISTIAN MOTHERS OF SMALL CHILDREN WORK OUTSIDE THE HOME?

This question was posed to me by a secretary who has a pre-teen daughter and is expecting a second child. (Whether my answer was a factor in her decision to stop work and devote full time to the home, I'll never know.)

I'd rather not open myself up to the label of male chauvinist, yet I know that my honest opinion will make me vulnerable. But simply stated, my answer to this question is, "No, I don't think Christian mothers of small children should work for profit in employment outside the home."

Obviously, there are exceptions. A widow may be forced to work in order to provide food for her children. A woman with special gifts may need to fulfill her obligations to herself and to society. But the mother I have in mind when answering this question is the average Christian woman whose husband has a reasonably adequate income and whose home includes several children. And again I say, "No."

What leads me to this opinion? In the creation story God declared, "It is not good that the man should be alone; I will make him a helper fit for him" (Gen. 2:18). The point is not that one spouse should be subservient to the other but that each should complement the other. Paul speaks of man and wife becoming one as Christ and the church are one (Eph. 5:31-32). This kind of unity requires total cooperation and involvement in the same basic purposes. However, it does not confuse the functions of each.

Women's lib advocates are convinced that women have borne the brunt of male discriminatory practices in almost every field of public endeavor. They say that confinement to the home and responsibility for raising children have robbed the woman of all opportunity for professional fulfillment. In the new rhetoric, staying home is the equivalent of treason to one's sex.

In an effort to halt discrimination on the basis of sex, government is everywhere encouraging female participation in the areas once thought to be the sole province of the male. Women are now state troopers, jockeys, politicians, administrators, and astronauts. A recent TV special applauded the androgynous personality (both male and female in one) as a goal to be achieved.

It is important at this point to remember that God's ways and judgments are under no obligation to agree with whatever the contemporary wisdom may decree. (For an outstanding presentation of the necessary conflicts between secular thinking and Christian thought, read Harry Blamires, *The Christian Mind*, SPCK). Secular thought, which builds upon naturalistic presuppositions, will inevitably arrive at positions which conflict with Christian thought. The role of the woman in current debate in no way alters the mind of God. Therefore, the believer must be careful how he interprets what God does decree in and through Scripture.

The Biblical position is that man and wife join in carrying out the will of God in this world as effectively as possible. In Paul's day this involved certain restrictions (I Tim. 2:11-14) as well as certain advantages (I Tim. 2:15: "saved through bearing children" should be interpreted to mean that the woman's significance in society is fulfilled and maintained through her role of giving birth to children and guiding them into productive adulthood). The crucial question today is not, Should women be employed as firemen and garbage collectors? but, Can society hold together if a generation of children grow up deprived of the continuing guidance of a mother who is there when needed?

Christians are under obligation to "train up a child in the way he should go." Surrogate parents, no matter how well intentioned, simply will not do. The Christian's philosophy of life is radically different from the secular world-view. If parents are not teaching their children Christian values, then society will implant and nurture all sorts of alien ideologies. The most important kind of teaching is that which arises spontaneously at unexpected moments. Mothers away at work have no way of taking advantage of these critical moments.

IS PAUL'S ADMONITION IN EPHESIANS 6:4, "FATHERS, PROVOKE NOT YOUR CHILDREN TO WRATH," TO BE TAKEN LITERALLY? WOULDN'T THIS DO AWAY WITH DISCIPLINE?

As a father of several teenage boys I have had this verse quoted me on more than one occasion. While it has always been in the spirit of good fun, it nevertheless has a little barb. A quick survey of the modern translations offers little comfort to the annoyed parent. Phillips says, "Don't overcorrect your children." Williams exhorts fathers to "stop exasperating [their] children." The New English Bible speaks of goading children to resentment. Apparently Paul meant what he said. Severe correction which angers the child is contrary to the teaching of Scripture. Phillips extends the verse (without textual support but in harmony with the larger context) by adding, "or make it difficult for them to obey the commandment," that is, "Honor your father and mother" (v. 2).

The Greek word translated "provoke" is *parorgidzō*, to make angry. It is compounded from a word which means to excite or to enrage. The father-child relationship is not to be such that a word of correction leads to resentment or anger. The responsibility for correction without antagonism lies squarely upon the shoulders of the father.

But doesn't this sort of approach lead to permissiveness? A number of social theorists do say that letting children have their own way was a major factor in producing the contemporary counter-culture. So, let us look at the context of Paul's statement. Fathers are not to provoke their children, BUT—and here we have the proper alternative—they are to "bring them up in the discipline and instruction of the Lord" (NASB). The apostle does not say, "Stop bugging your kids; let them do whatever they want." "Don't provoke" is in perfect harmony with "Bring them up in discipline and admonition." Correction, admonition, and warning are all necessary parts of raising children. "Don't provoke" does not mean "Don't correct." The trick is to carry out this responsibility without alienating the child.

It is easy to see that the correction and its reception depend upon the relationship between parent and child that has grown up over a period of many years. Parents who have lost or forfeited a meaningful relationship with their children are on thin ice when they begin to correct. But parents who have carefully and prayerfully nurtured this relationship will be able to admonish rather freely without provoking resentment. Child-rearing is much more of a full-time occupation than we are liable to suppose. Absentee parents discover after it is too late that what they have sown (disinterest and lack of attention) they are now reaping. Their children often become disinterested in the parent's values, life styles, and God. Discipline becomes virtually impossible because children who are emotionally rejected have little interest in establishing relations with parents who have neglected them. Parents tend to compensate with the heavy hand which in turn drives the child away. He may very well seek from his peers the acceptance that he doesn't get from parents, and this often leads into the world of drugs and sexual license.

Fathers are not to overcorrect their children. But they won't have to if a relationship of paternal and filial love exists. I know a boy of twelve who, when chided over his unwillingness to join his friends in a wrong course of action, answered the taunt, "You're afraid your Dad will hurt you," with the beautiful words, "No, I am afraid I will hurt my Dad." Here was a father who had learned how to encourage, correct, and admonish without provoking.

The tendency toward overkill is an indication of insecurity. Disciplinary overkill is an open acknowledgment of parental failure. It is not firmer discipline which is needed but parents whose very lives draw their children toward the right path. A boy who loves his father will, in the final analysis, want to be like him. In the excitement of youth he will not always act in accord with his father's deepest intentions, but then, do we as mature adult Christians always respond to our heavenly Father in perfect obedience?

WHAT ABOUT TV? WHAT LIMITATIONS SHOULD CHRISTIAN PARENTS PLACE UPON THEIR CHILDREN?

Television has brought a dramatic change into the life of modern society. Whatever its bane or blessing, you can be sure it is here to stay. Through TV, the whole world pours into our homes with a directness undreamed of several decades ago. It is unashamedly commercial. Programs live or die not by their merit, but by their ability to hold an audience. The great majority of what comes over the tube is evaluated strictly in terms of what it can do, not for the viewer, but for the sponsor. This alone ought to cause a parent to think twice before allowing his kids to watch whatever happens to be on tonight.

If the commercial basis of TV demands that writers give the people what they want, and if the Bible is right about the nature of man, then the Christian parent ought to be aware that what he and his children are viewing is likely to be in complete opposition to the Bible's basic presupposition: that man's greatest happiness is found in a living relationship to Jesus Christ.

The use of violence for "entertainment" is a matter of increasing concern among informed people. According to Duncan Williams in his controversial book, *Trousered Apes*, the three prominent themes in a culture which is disintegrating are sex, violence, and insanity. A Russian news release on the movie "Jaws" said it exploited a sense of fear, required no intellectual involvement, and was designed solely for profit.

WHAT DO YOU THINK ABOUT SEX EDUCATION IN THE LOWER GRADES?

The question of sex education in the public school has received much publicity recently. It appears that here is one more area where a public agency has decided it should take over what has always been a parental responsibility. Not that this responsibility has always been carried out: parents are usually a bit touchy on the subject. The argument is that since parents do not teach their children about sex, the school should. Otherwise they will learn about it from their poorly informed peers.

In my opinion there is considerable confusion about this issue. The word *sex* itself is used in different ways to denote different things. For our purpose let us distinguish between sex as the biological aspect of reproduction and sex as the mature and intimate expression of conjugal love.

In the latter sense, sex education belongs in the home. I would judge it inappropriate and offensive to discuss personal matters of this nature in a public forum. On the other hand, since the study of the human body is an essential division of biology, I would think that at an appropriate time the physiology of reproduction should be studied in the framework of the educational curriculum.

Just when and exactly how this understandably sensitive subject ought to be handled will be determined by responsible teachers and concerned parents. Generally speaking, biology is a high school subject. The apparent desire to introduce the sexual aspect of it at an earlier period reveals an administrative need to stay up with the latest educational fads.

A basic argument for early sex education ("Otherwise they'll learn it from their friends") rests upon the faulty assumption that man's sexual problems are rooted in his misunderstanding of the *biological* aspects of reproduction. This is obviously false. Modern knowledge of conception and birth does nothing to relieve the problem of promiscuity. Premature exposure to "sex education" which maximizes the similarities between animal and human reproduction is definitely harmful and may seriously impair a mature understanding of the unique quality of human sexuality.

OUR VACATIONS ALWAYS TURN OUT TO BE BIG HASSLES. SOMETIMES I THINK WE'D BE BETTER OFF TO STAY AT HOME. ANY SUGGESTIONS?

Yes, stay at home! We Americans tend to be compulsive in everything we do. We work so hard at having a successful vacation that it takes a couple of weeks back on the job before we are rested again. Pardon my reaction, but when I see a fully loaded camper with a motorcycle in front, a boat on top, and a dune buggy being pulled behind, I want to get away from the American scene. How about staying put in one spot, hiking with the kids or just doing nothing for a change? Recreation means *to create anew,* and this demands a distinct change of pace. Why not let the kids plan the entire vacation? You'll be surprised at their choices and probably save some money as well.

DO YOU THINK A CHRISTIAN PARENT SHOULD SEND HIS SON OR DAUGHTER TO A STATE UNIVERSITY?

Let me begin by listing what I believe to be the advantages and disadvantages of a secular university over against a Christian college (assuming that is the alternative). The average university has the advantage of being less expensive yet much better equipped. This is especially true in the sciences and in such non-academic areas as student centers and athletics. Universities bring to the campus each semester widely recognized authorities for special lectures and cultural events.

The greatest failure of the modern university is its inability to provide an integrated world-view which gives meaning and direction to the "pursuit of truth." In a recent address to the Association of American Colleges, Irving Kristol of New York University said, "We are all of us aware that university education in the United States today is in utter shambles. We have all seen bright, young high school graduates move on to our college campuses and, after only a relatively short period, display a feebler intellect, a less cultivated sensibility and a great vulgarity of soul than either God or their parents bequeathed to them." Part of the reason for this lamentable situation is that professional advancement (often spelled $) by research and publishing has lured the more able teachers out of the classroom and into the lab. In larger universities the undergraduate rarely has the privilege of direct exposure to those eminent professors whose names lend brilliance to the university's scholastic reputation.

Happily, the average Christian college finds it economically impossible to shield its best teachers from extensive exposure to the student body. It has the decided advantage of interpersonal relations within the academic community as a whole. On the minus side, the Christian college often develops an ingroup mentality which somehow allows its creative energies to be squandered on trivial concerns.

Although deciding which kind of college would be best must of necessity be based on the individual student, my own appraisal leads me to say that if I were primarily interested in the best *educational* experience, I would recommend a good private or Christian college. On the other hand, a relatively mature Christian young person might well find that his *spiritual* development would be enhanced by exposure to life on the secular campus—especially if a strong InterVarsity or Campus Crusade chapter is available.

HOW DO YOU EXPLAIN PAUL'S LOW VIEW OF MARRIAGE IN I CORINTHIANS 7?

No discussion of family life would be complete without reference to Paul's teaching on marriage. I can hardly deny that Paul appears to have a low view of marriage in the passage cited. In verse 9 he frankly grants that "it is better to marry than be aflame with passion." Later he counsels the unmarried not to seek marriage and reluctantly concedes, "But if you marry, you do not sin" (v. 28). Paul reasons that the married man is anxious about worldly affairs—specifically, "how to please his wife"—and is unable to give his undivided attention to the Lord (vv. 32-35). Verse 38 summarizes the apostle's position: "He who marries his bethrothed does well; and he who refrains from marriage will do better." This piece of advice is not liable to be received with any enthusiasm by the young in love!

Before we categorize Paul as an enemy of marriage we must take a careful look at the context of these statements. Are they universal axioms without qualifications or are there indications within the passage which suggest a specific interpretation? Two things are worthy of note. First, it is "in view of the impending distress [that] it is well for a person to remain as he is" (v. 26). The nature of this "impending distress" is clarified in the verses which follow: "The appointed time has grown very short" (v. 29), and "the form of this world is passing away" (v. 31). Paul believed that the return of Christ would take place within his own lifetime (cf. I Thess. 4:17) and therefore advises the Corinthian believers to avoid all worldly involvements which would divert their energies from serving the Lord.

Second, throughout this chapter Paul stresses that he is offering his own opinion rather than passing on a direct command of Christ. Verse 12 ("I [say], not the Lord") is representative of the tone of the chapter (cf. also vv. 6, 25, 40). While this does not mean that his statements are untrue, it does seem to place them in a special category. What a contrast in tone is a passage such as I Thessalonians 2:13 where he writes "When you received the word of God which you heard from us, you accepted it not as the word of men but as what it really is, the word of God."

A thoughtful reading of Ephesians 5:21-33 should dispel any lingering notion that Paul had a "low view of marriage." Husbands are to love their wives as Christ loved the church. Wives are to be subject to their husbands. (Note that in both cases each spouse is to adjust to the welfare of the other: that is exactly what the opening sentence says [v. 21]). This relationship of loving concern and gentle merging of identities becomes for Paul an appropriate expression of the mystery of Christ and the church. Nowhere will you find a higher view of marriage.

DO YOU FAVOR EARLY MARRIAGES?

A number of parents are faced with the problem of children wanting to marry at an early age. It has been said that youthful infatuation is called puppy love because it is the beginning of a dog's life! But what should we say about the young couple, strongly attracted to each other and wishing to marry?

As a general rule, I don't favor early marriages. But then, I don't favor late marriages either. The critical point in counseling young people who want to marry right out of high school (or before) is to help them realize that infatuation is not an adequate foundation for a lasting marriage. I do not mean to imply that there is anything wrong with romanticism. The person who has never had a "cloud nine" experience is that much the poorer. But unless romantic love deepens into a more mature relationship of personal affection it will wither and die.

Marriages are strengthened by the decision to mingle common sense with the desires of the heart. Love grows by addition, not subtraction. In a more mature love the romantic quality is not lost, but deepened and enriched by a fuller and far more satisfying dimension. As two lives become one, a new entity emerges which infinitely transcends all preparatory stages.

Early marriages are disadvantaged right from the start—the decision to marry is normally made before the young people can understand or appreciate by experience the deepening quality of genuine love.

WHAT ABOUT DIVORCE? ISN'T THIS THE BASIC REASON FOR THE BREAKUP OF FAMILY LIFE IN AMERICA?

Divorce has become one of the stark realities of contemporary life. In many states the divorce rate approaches, or even exceeds the marriage rate. However, divorce itself is not the cause, but rather the result, of a breakdown in the marriage relationship. Homes are broken long before the public and legal announcement of separation. Actually, in a great number of cases, what passes for marriage is little more than reluctance to declare by law a state of alienation which exists in fact. Renewed attention should be given to the problems which separate a man and wife, rather than to the legal restraints which keep them at the same address.

But to rephrase the question thus, "Does the increasing ease with which divorce may be secured undermine the stability of marriage?" I would have to answer, Yes. One attorney I know always delays appointments for those seeking to initiate divorce. He finds that a delay of several weeks often brings about a change of mind. A less scrupulous lawyer with an eye on the fee could encourage the step by his willingness to move ahead without delay. ("After all, my job is to handle the legal paperwork, you know; and who am I to interfere?")

When Moses required a "bill of divorcement" (Deut. 24:1 ff., cf. Matt. 5:31-32) it was to deter, not encourage, separation. Any requirement which prevents us from acting hastily against the best interests of all involved is good legislation.

On the more positive side our attention should be directed toward those problems which gradually undermine the relationship between man and wife. Petty though they often are, the cumulative effect of unresolved differences results in the erosion of love.

Marriage is God's divine intention for man. He said, "It is not good for the man to be alone. I will provide a partner for him" (Gen. 2:18). This partnership is developed and enriched by the mutual sharing in love of the experiences of life. That which inhibits the growth of this relationship is contrary to the will of God.

When Believers 4
Gather
To Worship

Pierre Berton writes in *The Comfortable Pew* that "the Christian philosophy and ethic has been shackled by its institutional chains" and that "in its desperate effort to preserve its established entity, the Church has become fossilized" (p. 115). To what extent this charge is true depends upon the life and vitality of each congregation.

The present chapter will discuss a number of issues related to the corporate life of the local church.

CAN A PERSON BE A CHRISTIAN WITHOUT GOING TO CHURCH?

This question suggests a number of possible analogies. Can a person be civic minded without belonging to a service organization? Can a person be a scholar without some relationship to an educational institution? Can a person be a father if he decides to live away from home? In other words, questions of this sort lack the kind of definition necessary for any sort of a precise answer. They are "Yes, but ..." questions. I suspect that the real question which lies behind the others is, "Do I have to follow through with the organizational implications of my commitment?"

A man's reasons for going to church are determined to some extent by his concept of the people of God. The greater the significance one sees in the corporate nature of the church the more one will want to gather with other believers. With the understanding that both the assembly and the individual are responsible for achieving certain goals, let me suggest three reasons for going to church:

(1) It is an opportunity for sharing spiritual truth and practical insight into Christian living. Paul told the believers at Rome that he longed to see them in order to impart some spiritual gift, and then quickly added, "that is, that we may be mutually encouraged by each other's faith, both yours and mine" (Rom. 1:11-12).

(2) It is an opportunity to rekindle the fires of personal devotion at the altar of corporate worship. Like an undisturbed and smoldering fire we tend to grow heavy with ash and lose our warmth. The disturbing action of Biblical preaching removes the residue of yesterday's burning, and the wind of the Holy Spirit encourages the flickering flame of personal devotion to again burn brightly.

(3) It is an opportunity for organized outreach into the world. Organization need not be the burial ground of the Holy Spirit. It is only intended to simplify the task and realize its goals in the most efficient manner. When organization serves the desires of the Holy Spirit, it increases the impact of His ministry.

The old saying that Christians are like porcupines on a cold night (they need each other for warmth but the closer they get together the more they stick each other) is not necessarily true. Being in Christ we are also "in one another." Corporate worship strengthens the bonds of unity which bind us together.

DO YOU HAVE ANY SUGGESTIONS FOR MAKING THE MORNING WORSHIP SERVICE MORE MEANINGFUL?

Granted, attendance at church is important. Many people agree in principle, but so often in practice routine takes over and the whole experience is just plain dull.

Most people would also agree that the primary purpose of the morning service is to bring about an experience of corporate worship. "O magnify the Lord with me, and let us exalt his name together" (Ps. 34:3) should be the heart-cry of everyone entering the sanctuary on Sunday morning. In the hour of worship men and women are led into the presence of God by prayer, song, and the proclamation of the Word. This inevitably issues in a renewed commitment to Jesus Christ and enthusiastic dedication to the privilege of world evangelism (Matt. 28:19).

Everything about the service ought to serve this basic purpose. But a church is also a social organization which of necessity has its housekeeping chores. Perhaps it would be best to keep to a minimum all those activities in the morning service which relate to running the program, and concentrate on creating an environment and opportunity for confrontation with God.

Perhaps the emphasis of many churches has been too much on the frailties of man and not enough on the sufficiency of God. Let us give God Himself the opportunity to speak. It is more important in our frenetic society than it ever has been before to be still and know that He is God. Planning the morning service with this in mind will require sensitivity, flexibility, and creativity.

MOST YOUNG PEOPLE SEEM TO THINK THAT THE SUNDAY MORNING PREACHING SERVICE IS NOT RELEVANT TO THEIR NEEDS. DO YOU HAVE ANY IDEAS ABOUT REVITALIZING THE CHURCH SERVICE WITH THE NEEDS OF YOUNG PEOPLE IN MIND?

First of all, it appears that the "problem" of the Sunday morning church service is not only a young people's problem. Discontent is expressed more openly by those who have little to lose by talking freely. Older people in the congregation have learned to put up with more and are willing to hang on and hope for a change. The young are more apt to just quit coming.

We should also distinguish rather carefully between relevancy and modernity. Confusion at this point leads people to believe that whatever is new and reflects that which is in vogue at the moment is by definition relevant. This is not the case. Modernity deals with the existing culture; relevancy has to do with basic human needs. Scripture is relevant because it is significant for modern man and his real needs. Using coke and crackers for communion is modern but not necessarily relevant. When people say that they want a relevant Sunday morning service they may be saying that they want it to be permeated with the spirit of the times. While this may be a good method of communication, especially with the younger set, it does not guarantee relevancy. The service will be truly relevant only if it speaks to the essential needs of man.

And the answer to relevancy is so close that we often overlook it. God is eternally relevant. When He speaks to the human heart He does it in the present tense. This is the mystery of preaching—that exposition of what God did and said in the past becomes God speaking in the present. If preaching is to be relevant it must be genuinely Biblical. Far too many worshipers go to church Sunday morning expecting to hear God's Word and come away discouraged because they have heard only the preacher. This happens in fundamental churches as well as liberal churches. The great need of the contemporary church is to hear God speak, and the role of the minister as he stands in the pulpit is to expound the Scripture in such a way as to allow God to speak. When God speaks it is relevant—both to the young and to the old.

The other part of the question has to do with specific activities in the service which will attract and hold the attention of the young. I believe Biblical preaching will do this. However, various changes in the format of the service may help as well. One suggestion is to make the sermon a "preliminary," leading up to the singing of several hymns which make the same basic point as the sermon. All too often we sing in order to "warm up" for the sermon. We even sing to allow time for the choir to make it down from the loft to the front seats. (An interesting pastime is to count the choir members as they go out the side door and again as they re-enter to take their seats in the congregation.) We can enter into singing more meaningfully once our hearts have been touched by a message from God. It is psychologically sound to involve the congregation as participants after their common experiences of hearing God speak.

A wide variety of practices can be easily developed by any pastor who will give time and thought to the problem. These changes, however, are of secondary importance. They may support relevancy but they do not make a message relevant. In a spiritual sense it is God who is relevant. When He speaks we are struck with the timelessness and relevancy of all eternal issues.

HOW MUCH TIME SHOULD I BE EXPECTED TO GIVE TO MY CHURCH AND YET AVOID NEGLECTING MY OWN FAMILY?

This problem is one that plagues almost every conscientious Christian who is actively committed to the work of God through the local church. The most apparent answer—just stop going so much—doesn't really solve the problem. On the one hand, we recognize our supreme obligation to the cause of Christ. We agree that a man cannot be a disciple of Christ unless he places discipleship above family loyalties (Luke 15:26). We admire greatly the unflagging zeal and tireless activity of the apostle Paul. We nod approvingly at his commendation of Epaphroditus who "nearly died for the work of Christ" (Phil. 2:30).

On the other hand, we agree in principle that in a very special way we are responsible for the well-being of our immediate family. We recognize that to "train up a child in the way he should go" (Prov. 22:6) cannot be accomplished *in absentia*. A verse like I Timothy 5:8 ("If any one does not provide for his relatives and especially for his own family, he has disowned the faith and is worse than an unbeliever") simply cannot be expunged from the Bible.

But let us examine ourselves. Are we using the time we do have at home for the enjoyment and welfare of the family? For many parents, home is a regrouping area where they lay out plans for the next sortie. The real center of their life is at work or with friends. Actually, home should be the one great reason for which other activities exist. It is not preparation for something taking place on the outside, but the reward for what is accomplished there.

Ten minutes of undivided attention given a child is better than several hours of just being around. Children don't need huge blocks of your time. Be available when your children want you and learn to enter into what interests *them*. If you've shown them how to patch a bicycle tire or listened with genuine interest to something that happened at school, your children probably won't miss you terribly if you are away for a while in the evening.

Do your best to telescope responsibilities away from home. Help your pastor find ways to streamline the operation of the church. When church committees honestly want to accomplish more in less time, they will. Parkinson's law, that work expands to fill the time allotted for it, is never more true than at a deacons' meeting.

It would seem, therefore, that a Christian's responsibilities lie in that sensitive balance between his best for the Lord as it relates to the local congregation and his best for the Lord in terms of family obligations. It is not so much a matter of competing loyalties as it is the interpretation of one supreme loyalty as it relates to two separate spheres of activity. Pray about your commitments; simplify your life as much as possible; do your utmost to make what you do do of significant value; and leave the rest to the Lord. At the judgment He will not call on your nominating committee for evidence against you. He knows your heart.

MY HUSBAND TELLS ME THAT ALL MONIES NOT EARMARKED FOR CURRENT LIVING EXPENSES SHOULD BE GIVEN TO THE CHURCH. IS THERE ANYTHING IN THE NEW TESTAMENT THAT TELLS US TO PUT AWAY FOR A RAINY DAY?

Verses such as "do not be anxious about tomorrow" (Matt. 6:34) are not intended to be taken as forbidding life insurance, savings accounts, retirement plans, etc. They relate to nervous anxiety about tomorrow which leaves the individual no time or energy to "seek first the kingdom of God and his righteousness" (Matt. 6:33).

Forfeiting today's spiritual opportunities for tomorrow's financial securities displays an appalling lack of confidence in God's ability to provide normal preparation for needs which arise as surely as the sun. Normal preparation is not only wise but also a Christian responsibility. The parable of the pounds (Luke 19:11-27) counsels wise investment. Paul teaches that if anyone does not provide for his own he is "worse than an unbeliever" (I Tim. 5:8). Adequate provision for tomorrow's exigencies cannot be equated with the "love of money [from which] all sorts of evils arise" (I Tim. 6:10, Weymouth).

WHY SHOULD I TITHE?

That's a straightforward question so let me give a straightforward answer. Because Christ died for you. If that isn't worth a portion of your earnings, then I don't know what is!

Paul put it more diplomatically in his second letter to the Corinthians. He said, "For you know the grace of our Lord Jesus Christ, that though he was rich, yet for your sake he became poor, so that by his poverty you might become rich" (II Cor. 8:9). He assured his readers that he did not want them burdened so that others could be eased, "but that as a matter of equality your abundance at the present time should supply their want . . . that there may be equality" (II Cor. 8:13-14). Earlier he had given the example of the Macedonian churches whose "extreme poverty . . . overflowed in a wealth of liberality" and admonished the Corinthian church to excel in the same gracious work (II Cor. 8:2, 7).

Tithing is not a New Testament requirement in the Old Testament sense. The New Testament expectation is giving out of a heart of thankfulness. Love that gives less than the legal requirement is only a caricature of love.

HOW CAN I ENCOURAGE MY SUNDAY SCHOOL CLASS (ADULT IN THIS CASE) TO ENTER INTO DISCUSSION?

James Stalker once said that a teacher has done nothing unless the mind of the student has been moved to independent inquiry. Participation is everywhere encouraged by educational theorists.

We must recognize that people respond most readily in an atmosphere of friendly rapport. No one wishes to express himself if he senses that his opinion—which is a delicate extension of his ego—will be treated unkindly or misrepresented. Be the kind of a leader whom the group will instinctively trust and to whom they will be willing to venture a partially formed opinion. Another suggestion is that you ask the kinds of questions which can be answered from the experiential background of the group. If you have just spent several hours boning up on the technical details of Paul's third missionary journey, don't expect your class to be able to recall all the detail which you have memorized. Let them add personal perspective to important and far-reaching issues.

IS THE DAY OF GREAT PULPIT ORATORY OVER?

I honestly believe that the day of the pulpit spellbinder is about over. The advent of television and the accompanying change from the "hot" to the "cool" (in the McLuhan sense) approach to communication has permanently altered the consciousness of most Americans. The changing patterns of authority in American life no longer favor the elevation of a single spokesman to the role of a "golden-mouthed" Chrysostom or a fiery Savonarola.

Nowadays leaders are considered fallible. Any pretense that this is not the case meets with considerable skepticism. Congregations want to be talked to as real human beings. Their needs are not met by flowery rhetoric or endless alliteration. Nor do they want to be shouted at. One preacher's son asked why daddy was always so mad when he got up to preach!

I also believe that people are hungry for the Word of God. Not long ago I sat in a huge tent in southern California with an audience of about three thousand (most of whom were under twenty-five) listening with open Bibles for an hour and a half to an excellent exposition of the entire book of Ezra (all ten chapters!). It was straightforward Bible study, unadorned by canned illustration or cute excursions into the land of trivia.

The day of ministerial histrionics is about over. The agonized pleading of professional shouters belongs to that frontier mentality which is rapidly becoming history. Let us address ourselves sincerely and intelligently to the task of telling people about what God has done for their salvation.

HOW CAN I KNOW IF I AM CALLED INTO THE MINISTRY?

In American church life the call to the ministry has all too often been understood as a highly personal and slightly mysterious experience. We are reminded that God chooses the low and despised to confound the wise, that Noah made a fool of himself by building the ark and preaching imminent catastrophe, and that the apostle Paul never could have passed the qualification exams for the mission field.

Yet not even Paul, that rugged individual of primitive Christianity, decided on his own to become a missionary. Acts 13:2 records that while the leaders of the church at Antioch were worshiping and fasting the Holy Spirit said to them, "Set apart for me Barnabas and Saul for the work to which I have called them." Then after fasting and prayer "they laid their hands on them and sent them off."

Elders and deacons in the local church could do a great service for God's people if they would *encourage* into the ministry young men who are obviously gifted by God for that particular role in the believing community, and at the same time *discourage* others who, in spite of their lack of the necessary gifts, are gravitating toward the pastorate.

In evaluating your own abilities, give careful attention to (1) your willingness to enter a life of self-discipline; (2) your personal delight in the Word of God; (3) your ability to communicate (not just talk) effectively; (4) your degree of optimism and the balance which characterizes your approach to life.

The church of Jesus Christ should have no vacancies for defeated individuals whose sermons are public projections of their own unsolved difficulties. It is help that we as a congregation need—not another session of pulpit-induced self-flagellation. To minister the "good news" that God was in Christ reconciling the world to Himself and that in Christ there is power to break the dominion of sin is an exalted calling. It demands men who have proven in their own lives that it is so and are gifted by God to proclaim it to others.

IS IT REALLY NECESSARY FOR A YOUNG MAN TO SPEND SEVEN YEARS OF HIS LIFE IN COLLEGE AND SEMINARY BEFORE HE GOES OUT TO PREACH?

Once a young person has decided that God wants him in the ministry, then the subject of academic preparation arises. Usually the choice is made between attending a Bible school which allows one to get into the field more quickly or spending a few additional years to take the route of college plus theological seminary.

Few would deny that there have been many successful ministers who never attended a theological seminary. In fact, some have not even finished college. But before we settle on the exception as the rule, consider the following points:

1. Practically all professions require considerable work beyond the four-year undergraduate program. In medicine and law the candidate spends four or more years in graduate and professional training before taking up his practice. All levels of teaching require additional graduate study. Unless the role of pastor is lowered to the level of general supervisor of religious activities, he must be allowed the opportunity for advanced training comparable to that of other professions.

2. The complexities of modern society with its ever-changing values require a level of spiritual and psychological insight, not to mention emotional security, which can scarcely be achieved apart from a serious program of studies beyond the undergraduate level.

3. A broad background in the liberal arts is generally considered the best possible preparation for a sympathetic understanding and appreciation of the deeper dimensions of life. To sacrifice this experience for an immediate involvement in "winning the lost" is, in the long run, an exceedingly poor choice.

The ministry requires a level of professional training commensurate with the role it plays in the life and destiny of man. We should do all within our power to provide theological preparation of the highest caliber for those who minister in the name of Christ.

SHOULD EVERY MINISTER HAVE A GOOD WORKING KNOWLEDGE OF GREEK?

A good share of a minister's preparation should be directed toward a comprehensive understanding of the Word of God. The power of the gospel does not rest in oratorical ability, but rather in God Himself who speaks through His Word. To be sure that it is God's Word, and not ours that we proclaim, it is necessary to know something about the original languages.

I am convinced that a working knowledge of the Greek New Testament makes sermons more Biblical, more interesting, and more rewarding. Among the many reasons for the study of Greek are:

1. It aids the twentieth-century interpreter in penetrating the cultural, religious, and linguistic barriers of the New Testament world. While the living Christ is ever contemporary, the written account of His death and resurrection is couched in an idiom remote from our own.

2. The more scholarly and influential New Testament commentaries are open for intelligent interaction only to those who approach them with a solid background in Greek.

3. It allows for the thrill of discovery! Even a relatively minor point of interpretation will come alive and glow with the warmth of divine illumination if the insight comes as a personal discovery.

Language study is hard work, but it pays great dividends. To those with sufficient dedication there are unique and priceless rewards.

I AM CONFUSED BY SO MANY PREACHERS AND TEACHERS SAYING SO MANY DIFFERENT THINGS. HOW CAN I KNOW WHO OR WHAT IS RIGHT?

I can genuinely sympathize with this frustration. The airways are full of "prophetic voices," each with a particular truth to drive home or an insight which must be shared. The Sunday marathon on the average Christian radio station is nothing short of a religious overkill. The problem is compounded by the sectarianism of Protestant Christianity, the tendency of believers to adopt favorites among the stellar conference heroes, and the ever-present tape recorder to expand the boundaries of the in group.

I believe the answer is to make a determined effort to find out exactly what Scripture says. There is no substitute for a day-by-day, unhurried exposure to the Word of God. The One who created us for fellowship in the first place can and will teach us, as we remain open and obedient in His presence. Those who know Christ in a personal way and have lingered long over the Scriptures will instinctively recognize error, no matter how it may be disguised in religious trappings.

In the final analysis, each one of us must choose between the alternatives. In the great essentials of the Christian faith there is broad agreement, which overrides denominational differences. Stay with these. Avoid sectarian bickering over fine points of doctrine which are of little significance and are unrelated to that quality of life to which all sound teaching must lead.

5

The Church
In The World

Jesus left His disciples with the mandate, "Go . . . make disciples"—*demonstrate the transforming power of divine life.*

How well has it been done? Does the average church on the corner resemble at all the ideal set forth in Scripture? Probably not. Yet, what would society be without the church? Are not its benefits felt throughout the entire structure of human society? Think of the origins of higher education in America, the hospitals, and the numerous other humanitarian enterprises which began as outreaches of the church.

The present chapter discusses a number of areas where the church and the world meet. There is no doubt that the church is in the world; the crucial question is how it is to relate itself redemptively to the world.

I RECENTLY HEARD A MAN SAY THAT THE CHURCH STANDS CONDEMNED FOR HER LACK OF BURDEN FOR THE LOST. DO YOU AGREE WITH THIS?

It is not news that the church frequently, if not regularly, expends her energies on peripheral concerns. Anti-establishment barrages such as Peter Berger's *The Noise of Solemn Assemblies* and Pierre Berton's *The Comfortable Pew* are painful reminders of our failures. All too often the cynical definition of the church as "a country club with a steeple" is an accurate one.

On the other hand, we must not envision the model church as a group of people groaning in travail under the oppressive burden of saving the lost. This neglects the clear teaching of Scripture that Christ's yoke is easy and His burden is light (Matt. 11:28-30). Unfortunately, the church has at times chosen the heavy burden of institutionalism instead of the light burden of gladly sharing the good news.

IS IT RIGHT FOR CHURCHES TO BUILD BIG BEAUTIFUL BUILDINGS WHEN FOREIGN MISSIONS ARE SO DESPERATELY IN NEED OF FUNDS?

I hope you will remember that in response to questions like this I can only offer an opinion, not provide an all-encompassing final answer. Circumstances vary so greatly that it is impossible to respond to a general question with a specific answer.

The usual argument put forward by those eager to build large churches is: (1) We can operate more effectively with a better building; (2) God's work deserves the best we can build; (3) People are more apt to join if we have a more attractive building; (4) A well-designed church is more conducive to worship.

Those opposed to building—and they are generally in the minority—say: (1) We ought not to spend so much on ourselves; (2) Other areas of God's work demand our resources; (3) The church is a gathering of redeemed individuals and where they meet is relatively unimportant.

It is helpful to keep in perspective the difference between the mission of the church and the methods it employs to carry out this mission. The mission of the church is to live redemptively in the world. This involves not only the proclamation of the gospel but also an actual demonstration of the transforming power of self-less love. Whether or not such a mission can be best accomplished with a bigger and better building—or any building at all for that matter—must be answered by each Christian as he prayerfully considers how God would have him use his tithe.

I am inclined to think that there is money both for necessary buildings and for foreign missions. I do not mean to say I support the thesis that buildings of any kind (especially ornate monuments to the creativity of an architect and the gullibility of people who unwittingly act as his patrons) are absolutely necessary to the fulfilling of the mission of the church in our day.

HOW AGGRESSIVE SHOULD CHRISTIANS BE IN EVANGELISM? SHOULD WE "LIVE THE LIFE" OR "BUTTONHOLE THE SINNERS"?

I have always been intrigued by Philip, the disciple of Jesus. Not simply because his name (in Greek) means lover of horses, but because of his straightforward and honest approach to life. The first three Gospels do no more than to list him with the rest of the disciples, but

John gives us four vignettes which reveal the man and his approach to evangelism.

When he was asked by Jesus where food could be bought to feed the five thousand (John 6), Philip replied that it would take more than two hundred dollars' worth of bread to give each person just a little (vv. 5-7). In John 12:20-22 it was to Philip that the Greeks came to inquire about an audience with Jesus. In John 14:8-9 it is Philip who requests of Jesus, "Show us the Father; that is all we need" *(Good News for Modern Man)*. These passages reveal that Philip was an uncomplicated man with no desires to impress. Apparently, Jesus chose to commit the early growth of the Christian church (in an era of growing hostility) to simple and honest men.

Let's return to Philip's first act of evangelism. In John 1:43 Jesus decides to leave Judea and go to Galilee. He finds Philip and invites him along as a traveling companion. Philip, realizing that Jesus is the prophet of whom Moses wrote in the Law, finds his friend Nathanael. Philip shares with him the good news that Jesus, the son of Joseph (the carpenter of Nazareth), is in fact the long-awaited deliverer.

At this point Philip runs into an obstacle. "Is it possible" objects Nathanael, "that out of *Nazareth* (such an insignificant village) something good should come?" Wouldn't Jerusalem with its temple and tradition be a more likely place?

Philip has several choices. He can take offense at Nathanael's refusal to take his word for it. Or, he can get involved in a long theological disputation about passages in the Old Testament which may or may not rule out the possibility that the Messiah could come from a small Galilean hamlet. Instead he answers, "Come and see." No amount of reasoned discourse will lead inevitably to the truth of revelation. Truth can only beckon; it cannot coerce.

A man commits himself to truth for three reasons. First, a true message has a drawing power all its own. If a man does not accept the truth, his refusal is not on the grounds that he genuinely questions its integrity. For example, the truth that love is better than hate is self-authenticating. It belongs to the universal and axiomatic structure of human existence. It needs no argument.

Second, truth is supported by the personal testimony of those who have experienced it and share their confidence with others. The simple "Come and see" is far more than an invitation. It declares that one is absolutely sure that when you meet the evidence you will be moved to share his conclusion. There is nothing frantic or defensive about the tone here; rather, there is a quiet confidence in the persuasive power of truth.

The third factor in a man's discovery of truth is his personal decision to respond affirmatively. There are pressures in both directions. In one direction is the drawing power of truth itself, the desire to forsake that sense of alienation which results from resistance to truth, and the power of the Holy Spirit. The opposite pressure, which would prevent a man from moving toward truth, is the deceptive lure of sin which promises what our lower nature seems to crave. Only the individual himself can decide in which direction to yield. Nathanael stands in the moment of decision: skepticism says, "Stay," but a longing for truth says, "Come and see." Nathanael came and his life was revolutionized.

Shall we "live the life" or "buttonhole the sinner"? The answer is, let us like Philip become traveling companions of Jesus. Once we are actually on our way, we can share the good news that Jesus is the promised deliverer. As this message confronts others with the necessity of decision, we can then with a quiet and joyful confidence invite them to "Come and see."

WHAT DO YOU THINK OF SOME OF THE MORE SENSATIONAL METHODS BEING USED TODAY TO SPREAD THE GOSPEL?

We live in a culture which has been shaped by the magic of Madison Avenue to a greater extent than most would care to admit. The ad man is today's Pied Piper, leading great crowds to this product or that. It seems logical to ask, Why shouldn't a method that works in business be employed in the cause of Christ? Most of my knowledge of avant-garde religious experiments comes via the news media rather than personal involvement. And my opinion remains open for revision—as all opinions should.

In the Book of Acts certain precedents are established for carrying out the great commission. And I would assume that the methods employed by Paul also bear the divine imprimatur. This is obviously not to suggest that the contemporary church must operate within the limits imposed by life in the first century. But the degree of appropriateness of Paul's activities in his day ought to be matched by an appropriateness in our own day.

As we study Paul, we learn that he adapted himself to his audience: he became "all things to all men" (I Cor. 9:22). Is the contemporary church adapting its methods so it gains a hearing among the unsaved? Paul was willing to be excommunicated from the religious establishment. How many creative ideas today are smothered by the disapproval of the body ecclesiastic?

The activities which characterized Paul's ministry grew out of the faith which he proclaimed. The gospel is "good news of a great joy" (Luke 2:10) and the way it is told ought to be commensurate with its content. Good news is for telling, not for the personal delight of the cloistered few.

It seems to me that common sense can guide a person in determining when his method of spreading the good news is in poor taste. But good taste doesn't mean blandness. While bombing Wall Street with tracts wrapped in multi-colored cellophane or announcing on bumper stickers that God is alive may not be methods that appeal to all the saints, at least such approaches don't err on the side of unimaginative quiescence and dull routine.

WHY ARE MANY ARTICLES IN RELIGIOUS PERIODICALS CRITICAL OF EVANGELICAL CHRISTIANITY?

The passing of time inevitably affects every social movement in two ways. The first could be called the Law of Accretion, or growth by extraneous addition. Huge organizations whose spectrum of concern is as broad as society itself often began with a single good idea. The phenomenal expansion of the role of government in the last third of the century is a marked example. (Federal expenditures in 1970 alone were greater than the total from the founding of the nation through the mid-30s.) The second law could be called the Law of Complexity; that is, every social movement grows increasingly complex in direct ratio to its size.

Although the Christian faith is far more than a social movement it is nevertheless affected by the many pressures which come to bear on other social groupings. Thus it has not been immune from what we have called the laws of Accretion and Complexity. From a simple movement of Galileans who had seen their leader crucified and come to life after three days, there has developed a universal religious faith. Two thousand years of church history gives record of countless divisions, rebirth of dormant segments, and unbelievable change in customs and (in the broadest sense of Christendom) beliefs.

Even within the evangelical branch of Christianity—those who hold Scripture to be an authentic and reliable record of God's redemptive concern for man—there are serious differences. For some, communion involves the real presence of Christ in the elements, for others it is merely symbolic. Some chant the liturgy of previous centuries, others liven up their gatherings with, "Give me a J! Give me an E!" etc. Some resist the adornment of the "world," others use it as a vital part of their witness for Christ.

These differences which have grown up over the years tend to separate people and should be the subject of open discussion. One function of a religious periodical is to encourage its readership in an attitude of continual appraisal of its religious heritage. The purpose is not to find fault but to redirect oneself to the essentials of Biblical faith. Since man is by nature a myth-making creature, he needs a certain amount of debunking to keep him honest. Since unlearning is always more difficult than learning, he resists correcting the assumptions and practices which he learned from youth.

Historic Christianity has inherited a great tradition. Its adherents have grown up realizing the importance of a personal knowledge of Christ, the role of Scripture in directing faith and practice, and the urgent mission of the church to make disciples. Along with these central themes, however, have come other items of less significance. (Man seems to move naturally to the trivial.) Far more time is spent on questions of dress and conduct than upon the sovereignty of God. Not that such matters are unimportant or without guiding principles in Scripture; it is only that in the extreme they lose their relevance and dwindle off into a sort of dead legalism. Where this happens a fertile field opens for the professional debunker to exercise his art. While his contribution is important, of course, he runs the danger of taking too much personal pleasure in exposing the inconsistencies of his "less informed brethren."

More than once I have probably been guilty of creating theological and cultural straw men for the express purpose of knocking them down. When a writer is seized by the zeal to reform, he normally overstates his case. What is needed is balance between information by analysis and encouragement by positive direction. It is usually easier to find something wrong with the status quo (that's Latin for "the mess we are in") than to suggest some positive remedy. Most difficult of all is to demonstrate by one's own life how well a solution works.

ARE THE TEACHINGS OF JESUS SUPRACULTURAL? CAN WE PREACH THE GOSPEL ON THE FOREIGN MISSION FIELD WITHOUT WESTERNIZING THE PEOPLE THERE?

It is obviously impossible to equate Christianity with Western culture. Christianity's origins are in the East; it is the fulfillment of God's self-revelation within a Semitic society. Therefore, the teachings of Scripture must be interpreted from within the Judaic cultural milieu.

In our zeal for world evangelization we often overlook this very point. Just as the Judaizers of Paul's day insisted that Gentiles must become "Jews" before they could become Christians, we leave the impression that people of other nations must become Westernized in order to be saved. Nothing could be further from the truth; this reflects an overweening provincialism on our part. Christ came to save man from *sin*, not from any particular culture.

But I do not mean to deny that salvation will alter the way a man lives—the redeeming presence of the living Christ is bound to turn life upside down. I do deny the often tacit assumption that becoming a Christian obligates the foreign convert to adopt the religious mores of the Western world.

HOW FAR OUGHT WE TO GO IN MAKING THE GOSPEL RELEVANT TO MODERN MAN?

We are living in a day when contemporary society is under assault. The standards and values which a quarter of a century ago were almost taken for granted are being subjected to re-examination. And, they are being discarded at an alarming rate. The Establishment is pictured not only as socially irrelevant but as the enemy of human values. In this climate of revolt the church has not escaped criticism. From without there is scathing denunciation and within there is agonizing self-appraisal.

The banner carried by this growing army of the ecclesiastically disenchanted is "Make It Relevant." Nothing is too far out to be "in." At a summer youth camp potato chips and coke served as the elements for communion. Jesus of Nazareth is described as though he came from the inner city, was an arbiter in the management-labor struggle, led peace marches and lobbied for better housing.

I would not for a moment suggest that the risen Lord is unconcerned with human suffering and social injustice. My only concern is that, in our effort to "make the gospel relevant," we do not unwittingly transform it into something which it is not. The relevancy of the gospel (we do not *make* it relevant) lies precisely in the fact that it relates to man's fundamental problem—the problem of alienation from God. Until this is settled, all attempts to patch up the cracking seams of society are doomed to fail—they constitute a holding action at best.

If by relevant we mean *socially acceptable*, then we have headed down a blind alley. Paul states it succinctly in I Corinthians 1:23, "We proclaim a Christ who was crucified—an idea that is revolting to Jews and absurd to the heathen" (Goodspeed). The gospel is power and wisdom only to those who believe.

There are ways that Christian groups are attempting to reach out to modern man. For some this goes no further than capitalizing on the abilities of a converted entertainer. For the more avant-garde it may involve a jazz service or "folk happening." The text usually quoted to support these endeavors is I Corinthians 9:22, "I have become all things to all men, that I might by all means save some."

The good news proclaims a once-for-all historical event—the death and resurrection of Jesus Christ. It is pegged in history forever; it will never change. But, since proclamation involves communication, it must inevitably be cast in the idiom of modern man. We must be careful not to allow the form adopted to alter either the content or the overall spirit of the message.

Most evangelical enterprises guard the first (the content) but play havoc with the second (the spirit). Martin Kahler wisely remarked, "Paul indeed stated that he wanted to be a Jew to the Jew and a Greek to the Greeks, but he refused to be a miracle worker among the Jews or a cultural messiah among the Greeks."

SHOULD CONSERVATIVE CHRISTIANITY DIRECT ITS EFFORTS TO SAVING SOULS OR BROADEN OUT AND BECOME CONCERNED ABOUT SOCIAL ISSUES?

Some evangelicals feel that the conservative wing of the church has been so absorbed in winning the lost that it has failed to give adequate attention to the broader needs of society. But let me start from the premise that it would be impossible to have a regenerate society apart from regenerate individuals. This narrows the question down a bit to: How can we best bring about the regeneration of individuals?

A simply stated answer is, Preach the gospel. Some would say this is the total task of the church. Others insist that salvation's redeeming influence must pervade society and bring pressure to bear on all forms of injustice and inequality. Theologian Walter Rauschenbusch, the leading exponent of the social gospel in America, pointed out over a half century ago that the individualistic gospel failed to recognize that the social order is at least partly responsible for the sins of all individuals within it. He strongly emphasized the role of society in the transmission of sin (cf. *A Theology for the Social Gospel*, pp. 57-68).

While conservative biblical scholarship does not consider personal insight and social observation on a level of authority with Scripture, it should nevertheless give renewed attention to the *ethical implications* of the faith. Salvation is far more than securing entrance into heaven —it also involves the transformation of egocentricity into altruism. The idea of a saved person unconcerned about a social environment is ludicrous, since that environment greatly influences the effectiveness of the gospel.

The gospel is the good news that God has entered His creation to redeem man. When one accepts this premise, he is thrust into the mainstream of life. And, he will necessarily be deeply committed to the issues of life which relate to the total existence of all men.

IS CIVIL DISOBEDIENCE APPROPRIATE FOR CHRISTIANS SUFFERING UNDER AN UNJUST LAW?

Civil disobedience, in its historic sense (Thoreau wrote his famous essay on the subject in 1849), is the willful violation of a specific law in order to test the validity of that law before the courts of the land. It involves the willingness to pay the price for violation if the courts uphold the law.

However, it is important to distinguish between civil disobedience and plain lawlessness. Looting, obstructing the rights of others, personal injury, etc., may well stem from frustration and social injustice, but they represent a rejection of the principle of law and a movement toward anarchy. The intention of law is maximum freedom for the individual in a social setting. The denial of this principle leads man back to the jungle. Charles Rhyne has written, "Our personal and property rights and the future of the Republic cannot be left to the hands of a white man clutching a rifle in the toilet of a Memphis flophouse or to the hands of a black man clutching a Molotov cocktail in the nation's capital."

Civil disobedience, however, (as opposed to lawlessness) is appropriate for any man suffering under an unjust law. Maximum justice is the intention of the law and its statutes need constant modification to achieve that goal in our changing society.

The crucial question is how this change is to be brought about. History does not support the thesis of those who advocate a massive display of lawlessness. Eric

Severeid has pointed out that violence and coercion have always led to more violence and coercion. A society can strengthen its essential cohesive element by humane and rational reconstruction, not by an assault upon its only hope. In this process of renewal, civil disobedience can play a constructive role, but the forces of anarchy must be rejected.

DO YOU THINK THE CHURCH OUGHT TO GET INVOLVED IN POLITICS?

The church by definition is the *ekklēsia*, "those who have been called out." This fact has led some to espouse a cultural isolationism which cuts every unneccessary tie with the world and its ongoing operation.

A large segment of contemporary Christianity does feel that the church should get involved in politics. But only a starry-eyed idealist could fail to see that pressure, expediency, and compromise play a major role in the crucial political decisions of the day. "Rhetoric is meaningless!" cries the religious activist. "The future belongs to those who are able to muster the courage to act on their convictions." The reluctance of the church to speak out in the past about glaring social injustices strengthens the religious activist's determination to in fact *be* the "salt of the earth." The current secularization of society convinces him that God is where the action's at—in the local precinct, a march for peace, or labor-management negotiations.

While active concern for the welfare of man is commendable, there is some question that Jesus ever intended His kingdom to be advanced by political action. Everywhere He insists upon a transformation of the inner man as the *sine qua non* for a renewed society. Although He expended a tremendous amount of time

and energy in healing the sick, never did He allow anyone to imagine that physical suffering was man's basic
problem. There is no reason to believe that the role of
the church in today's world should be essentially different from what it was in the first century. The body of
Christ is to live in the world in such a way as to draw
others into an experience of the redeeming love of God.
Only when this is kept central can political activity exist
as a proper secondary concern.

IS IT POSSIBLE FOR A CHRISTIAN TO BE SEPARATE FROM THE WORLD AND STILL VERY MUCH IN IT?

That the Christian should be separate from the world in
which he lives is the strong thrust of a number of Scriptural passages. After asking a series of rhetorical questions (e.g., "What fellowship has light with darkness?"),
each calling for the answer, "None at all!" Paul quotes
the word of the Lord to Isaiah: "Come out from them,
and be separate from them," in support of his teaching
on the separated life (II Cor. 6:14-18). And John, the
beloved disciple, admonishes, "Do not love the world or
the things in the world. If any one loves the world, love
for the Father is not in him" (I John 2:15). Peter writes,
"As he who called you is holy, be holy yourselves in all
your conduct" (I Peter 2:15).

That ought to just about settle the question of the
relationship of the believer to the "crooked and perverse
generation" (Phil. 2:15) in which he lives. But let's add
one more passage. Speaking of the sons of disobedience
upon whom the wrath of God comes, Paul counsels the
Ephesian Christians, "Do not associate with them" and
in their works of darkness, take no part, "but instead
expose them" (Eph. 5:6-11).

But how can we witness to people unless we are where they are? Ought we not to minimize our differences so they will feel comfortable with us and willing to share their problems? Besides, didn't Jesus mix with sinners—even prostitutes? If we are judgmental and unsympathetic, won't we turn them off? Besides, didn't Paul also tell the Corinthians that although he had written not to associate with immoral men, he had not meant the immoral of this world, since in that case they would have had to be taken out of this world (I Cor. 6:9-10)?

So, is it a toss-up? Does Scripture counteract Scripture leaving us without direction in this critical issue? Are we in an ethical stalemate?

I think not. Let's look at the collage of arguments that support the position of maximum identification with the world. (Other arguments could probably be added, but those mentioned are the ones most often set forth.)

First, is it really true that we can share the claims of Christ most effectively with a person by making sure he is comfortable in our presence? Should we be sure that our "good news" doesn't touch his conscience or affect his composure? Not for a moment am I suggesting a holier-than-thou attitude. Nor can we countenance either the religious snob or the plaster paris saint. Those are not the alternatives.

But the message of the cross, Paul says, is a *skanda-lon*, a stumbling block (I Cor. 1:23). Jesus told His disciples that as the salt of the earth, should they lose their saltness, they would be good for nothing (Matt. 5:13). One of the things which the Holy Spirit does is to *convict* the world of sin (John 16:8). None of this suggests that an unrepentant sinner will be especially comfortable in the presence of a child of God. I am not suggesting that we should refuse to build bridges of kindly concern across which the redemptive message of Christ can travel. I am only saying, Don't be surprised if Christian witnessing makes your non-Christian friend uneasy.

Second, what about Jesus and His friends? The Pharisees and scribes gathered for the feast in the house of Levi complained, "Why do you eat and drink with tax collectors and sinners?" To which Jesus replied, "I have not come to call the righteous, but sinners to repentance" (Luke 5:29-32.)

Who were these "sinners"? Were they the profligates of Jesus' day? The vile and immoral dregs of society? Hardly. They were simply the common people of the land, the Am Ha-ares, who did not observe the Law in detail. There is no support for the position that Jesus chose for His companions the lowest stratum of human society.

In the house of Simon He allowed a woman of questionable moral character to kiss His feet and anoint them with ointment. But note that whatever she had been before, she left forgiven of her sins (Luke 7:36-50). Jesus doesn't call us to avoid at all costs the sinner seeking forgiveness in Christ. At the same time He doesn't call us to become like those who need to be changed.

Finally, what about Paul's acknowledgment that to escape association with the immoral of this world would require getting out of the world? The answer is not far from hand. The *kind* of association Paul is talking about is the normal and natural result of living in the same world everyone else does. If the butcher, the baker, and the candlestick maker all happen to be agnostics, it doesn't follow that we should become vegetarians who refuse bread and live in dark houses. What the New Testament doctrine of separation means is that we should not share in their unbelief. Neither should we try to build profound relationships with those who take as a basic premise that God doesn't exist or that He doesn't matter.

The best method of evangelization is to demonstrate by our daily walk the deep satisfaction of having surrendered our lives to Christ. If the Bible is true—and it is—men outside Christ who are seeking Him want to see models of what the Christian life is like.

Life In America

6

This chapter treats inquiries which relate specifically to this world and this country. It discusses the trends of contemporary society. What should the Christian do about the maelstrom of secular ideologies and practices which he believes threatens the well-being of life in America? In other words, is there a Christian perspective on social organization and governance? How should this direct those who want "In God We Trust" to continue as a national motto?

IS LIFE IN AMERICA COMING APART AT THE SEAMS?

There is little doubt that in the last decade or so contemporary America has entered into a period of unprecedented cultural revolution. In *The Greening of America*, Charles Reich heralds the imminent demise of the corporate state and welcomes the new consciousness that is sweeping the country. Less optimistic is Lewis Yablonski, who says in *The Hippie Trip* (p. 320) that

97

the present counter-culture is the first American social movement to totally reject the American social system. The results of an extensive poll of the social, ethical, and political attitudes of college students (Daniel Yankelovich, *The Changing Values on Campus*, 1972) supports the thesis that there is indeed a fundamental revolution of values taking place today.

For example, only one student in four regards casual premarital sex relations as morally wrong. Attitudes towards war as an instrument of national policy or as an expression of patriotism have changed dramatically. Over fifty percent of the students polled believed that there is only one justification for going to war—to counteract aggression from without. Students ranked religion, patriotism, beauty, and money as the least important values in their personal lives. (Love and friendship stood at the top of their lists.) Thirty-four percent of those surveyed were convinced that marriage is obsolete.

This revolution in values is seen most dramatically in the quest for sexual freedom. The Yankelovich study indicates that forty-one percent of the students polled believe that the interchange of partners among married couples is acceptable and seventy-four percent see nothing wrong with relations between consenting homosexuals. Readers of *Time* were recently exposed to the naked truth about uninhibited cinematic sexploitation in a cover story on Marlon Brando's performance in "The Last Tango in Paris." A liberated society accepts frontal nudity as R-rated and anything goes in movies rated X. Has Copenhagen with its two hundred pornography shops, sixty-five pornomats, and seventy-five places where one can watch "live" sexual intercourse (according to Jean-Paul Lauret in *The Danish Sex Fairs*) become our model?

One of the disheartening aspects of this revolution in values is that the organized church often appears to be on the wrong side. In an article entitled "The New Commandment: Thou Shalt Not—Maybe," *Time* reported that a Committee on Family Life of a major denomination issued a resolution implicitly condoning sex for single persons, homosexuals, and unspecified "other styles of interpersonal relationships" (Dec. 13, 1971). It also reported that six Christian education executives of another major denomination have drawn up a statement maintaining that sex is moral if the partners are committed to the "fulfilling of each other's personhood."

Back to the question: Is America coming apart at the seams? That we are in the throes of a cultural revolution cannot be denied. Whether the change taking place is beneficial or detrimental depends upon where you stand on the issues of personal and public morality. The young swinger would say that it is high time our repressive and guilt-ridden society got rid of its hang-ups and began to affirm life. The Christian who is committed to the Biblical ethic as a revelation of God's will must judge the value revolution with alarm. It should not, however, take him by surprise. Paul wrote of times of stress which will come in the last days when men will be arrogant, disobedient to parents, unholy, profligates, reckless, lovers of passion (II Tim. 3:1-4). While it would be extreme to say that all social change in America today is away from Christian principles, it is nevertheless true that the constant shaking of the foundations is moving the next generation closer towards the final collapse of human society.

IF SOCIETY IS ALWAYS GOING TO THE DOGS, HOW COME IT ISN'T THERE YET?

I've often wondered about this. It is obvious that in some areas man is worse off than he was in the previous generation. Most would agree that the disintegration of the structures of authority in contemporary society has resulted in an upsurge of criminal behavior. The current revolution in sexual mores looks far more like Romans 1 than Romans 8. Apparently, things are bad and getting worse.

But the way the question is stated seems to imply that is all an illusion. How could we have been on the way down so long and not arrived? The argument is not without force, especially when one recalls that the first parents not only rebelled against God (in a social and economic paradise, it should be noted) but their first son was a murderer. From that beginning the only way for the human family to go would be up!

A partial answer to the question is that while society is always "going down" in some ways, it may be "going up" in others. Perhaps it is our own sinful human nature that causes us to focus on the dark side of life. If we look back to that era when personal relationships between the sexes were more restrained (as a general rule), we are apt to find a greater amount of exploitation and social injustice. Are not the struggles of modern society to make equal opportunity a reality rather than a pious slogan indicative of a "rise" in social ethics?

HAS SOCIETY MADE ANY REAL MORAL PROGRESS SINCE THE DAY CAIN KILLED ABEL?

According to the historian Will Durant (who, with his wife Ariel, recently published "The Age of Napoleon," volume eleven of their Story of Civilization series), history has been filled with alternation of pagan and puritan epochs.

The contemporary period greatly resembles the Roman Empire in the latter half of the second century when, after having reached its height, it began to crumble. Durant states that the similarities between the two periods are "great wealth, great freedom, loss of religious faith, and an over extension of world-wide avenues of commitment."

Few social historians would argue with this analysis. Wealth has extended freedom, but unfortunately it carries with it a narrowing of outlook (the result of concentration upon acquisitions) which makes the intelligent use of freedom less likely. Without intelligence, freedom becomes chaos.

Durant also holds that our moral code has withered, since there is no longer any all-seeing deity to keep us in tow. The family structure has broken down, with the result that man grows more violent. To make things even worse, modern science has placed in our hands the instruments of ultimate self-destruction.

Most Christians will agree with Durant's analysis of the state of Western civilization. Technologically, we have progressed at a remarkable rate (even though some of the by-products of "progress" are causing concern, i.e., pollution, waste of natural resources, high level of psychological stress, etc.). But morally? Well, that's another question.

Most Christians will not agree that America's excesses will lead to its cure. Based on the observation of the alternation between pagan and puritan epochs, Durant feels that when we get sick of the excesses of one style of life we will be drawn to the opposite style. Hence, Durant claims that moral decay leads to moral health.

Nations do change over a period of time, and some of these changes are for the better. But it is not necessarily true that excess in one direction automatically produces its opposite. Many other variables enter the picture. The Christian believes that the will of God and the prayers of His children are significant factors in the direction of society. Believers acknowledge God's promise to Solomon, that "if my people who are called by my name humble themselves, and pray and seek my face, and turn from their wicked ways, then I will hear from heaven, and will forgive their sin and heal their land" (II Chron. 7:14).

The genuinely secular historian, of course, must rule God out as an active participant in history. What happens must always find its explanation within the material universe. Durant is quoted as saying "I am a descendant of a monkey . . . and so I understand the instincts we suffer from—violent pugnacity, limitless acquisition, indomitable sexual desire." He has indeed provided us with a succinct statement of the ills of natural man. Whether he arrived at this insight by being a part of the evolutionary process is another matter.

Yet Durant has hope. "Any civilization that can produce a Christ, a Moses, a Plato, a Spinoza, a Shakespeare, a Beethoven—well, it can't be all bad." He trusts that we can work our way out of the mess—he confesses that at age ninety he has lost his faith in "the wickedness of mankind."

The Christian is also a realist. He accepts the facts of human history as they stand. But he differs with the secular historian in where to find a cure for society's malaise. He believes in salvation in the widest sense but refuses to base his optimism on such questionable grounds as the historical phenomenon of an occasional genius. He believes in a brighter future because Christ died that man might have life more abundant. The One who holds the future is infinitely good and rewards the faith and obedience of those who put their confidence in Him.

I KEEP HEARING ABOUT WHAT A PERMISSIVE SOCIETY WE LIVE IN. IS THIS REALLY SO OR IS IT JUST ANOTHER THOUGHTLESS SLOGAN?

Slogans are condensed generalizations. As such, they are open to considerable abuse. But when understood as slogans, with full awareness of their susceptibility to abuse, they act as convenient tools in popular discourse. The reference to a "permissive society" is by no means incorrect just because the expression itself has become contemporary jargon.

Few would deny that in a general sense ours *is* a permissive society. This is not necessarily a moral judgment. The industry and creativity of one generation has made it possible for parents to give children the fruits of affluence. That "unearned fruit" is neither delectable or desirable is the lesson we are now learning.

In his excellent book, *Reality Therapy*, Dr. William Glasser makes it plain that one of man's basic needs is to feel worthwhile to himself and to others. No one ever felt worthwhile on the basis of what he received. This simple truth ought to help Christian parents to give their children the opportunity to "earn their own way" in as many of life's situations as possible. Otherwise we frustrate them in the fulfillment of one of the two basics (according to Glasser) necessary for emotional health and stability.

WHAT DO YOU THINK ABOUT THE WATER-GATE AFFAIR?

One problem with writing on a current political event is the time lapse before it appears in print. But that isn't the only problem. The events which the media force upon our attention day by day are but surface manifestations of issues which lie much deeper and call for serious interpretation. To further complicate the matter, interpretation is by definition subjective. Issues such as freedom, responsibility, courage, and love can neither be analyzed in a test tube nor verified on our most sensitive scales.

Watergate itself was a surface eruption on the body politic which dramatizes what Scripture has always taught—that from the moral failure in Eden to this present day, a poison called sin has been surging through the bloodstream of mankind. If Adam aspired to an autonomy which would deny his Creator full sovereignty, and if Cain determined that his own position in life would be enhanced by denying his brother the right to live, then we should not be surprised if man in the twentieth century finds it difficult to withstand the temptations of power. Reinhold Niebuhr often said that democracy is the preferable form of government because, considering the nature of man, it provides for society the most effective method of check and balance to keep the abuse of privilege to a minimum.

But doesn't such an appraisal lead to a dreary pessimism? Is man no more than another species in the world of tooth and claw?

Two things should be noted. First, in addition to being a rebel, man is also a being made in the image of God, capable of remarkable acts of self-denial and altruism. Men still jump fully clothed into lakes to save total strangers. They often share what little they have with those who have nothing. An ingrained self-concern and a strange but wonderful self-forgetfulness coexist in contradiction. Flashes of what God intended man to be illumine most unexpectedly the darkness of what a history of self-centeredness would lead us to expect. Man, the moral schizophrenic, leaves us just enough evidence of his potential greatness that we are unable to declare him devoid of goodness.

Second, God has not given man up. The incarnate Christ makes it possible for man to have a new nature. Union with God provides a source of supranatural power to overcome the downward drag of a fallen human nature. God allowed his Son to suffer the punishment for man's sin in order to restore the divine intention for humanity in the lives of those who believe.

Watergate is a symbol that this divine intention has not been realized in society as a whole. Watergate is a reminder that our social bloodstream still contains the same debilitating poison that accounts for a history of sorrow, bloodshed, and frustration. It should also remind us all—even those who profess the Christian faith— that we are too often part of the problem rather than convincing examples of the cure.

SHOULD A CHRISTIAN BE MORE PATRIOTIC THAN HIS UNBELIEVING NEIGHBOR?

In order to prevent misunderstanding, this term requires careful definition. The Concise Oxford Dictionary defines a patriot as "one who defends or is zealous for his country's freedom or rights."

Patriotism is not jingoism—an extreme nationalism marked especially by a belligerent foreign policy. It is, rather, wholehearted support of the basic ideals upon which a country is founded. A definition of patriotism would also include devotion to those fundamental moral principles which support and direct the national life.

With this as a background let us look at patriotism in America. Few would deny that the national climate has undergone a radical change in the past thirty years. On Monday morning, December 8, 1941, immediately after the bombing of Pearl Harbor, every young man in the small college I was attending went downtown to offer his services to the Army, Navy, or Marine Corps. To have reacted in any other way would have been moral cowardice. Resistance to military aggression was the appropriate patriotic response.

But thirty years later, many of these same young men, now fathers, were hoping against hope that their sons would not be drafted. Some were counseling how to avoid military service, and others were providing carfare to Canada. What had happened in that span of time? Had patriotic men become unpatriotic? Or is it possible that genuine patriotism was attempting to call a nation back to those fundamental moral principles which were viewed as having been violated by continued involvement in Vietnam?

It seems to me that loyalty must always be loyalty to the truth. One of the duties of a friend is to correct a colleague whose actions violate the accepted code of conduct. To go along with a breach in social responsibility on the basis of "friendship" is to pervert the very meaning of the word. After correcting the church at Galatia, Paul asked, "Have I now become your enemy by telling you the truth?" (Gal. 4:16). To acquiesce to the policies of one's nation without regard for the fundamental principles of justice is not true loyalty.

It is the mentality of the unthinking servant to voice approval of whatever is done by his superiors. But America's system of government was not based on a serf-master concept. It was, instead, built upon the idea of a community of free and equal patriots who believed that free men were capable of rational self-government. I am saying that criticism is a necessary ingredient in a free society and that its absence ultimately guarantees some sort of totalitarian control.

Back to the question. Should a Christian be more patriotic than his unbelieving neighbor? In the sense that a Christian is committed to the truth, to justice and self-sacrifice, the answer is, Yes. Having been redeemed by Christ and empowered by the Spirit, should he not play a leading role in setting the standard of true patriotism?

While the unbeliever desires freedom and justice for personal and social reasons, the Christian longs for them as an expression of the nature of God and His redemptive involvement in the world. In this sense the Christian should assuredly be a genuine patriot.

HOW IMPORTANT IS IT THAT PERSONS HOLDING POSITIONS OF LEADERSHIP IN PUBLIC OFFICE MAINTAIN A HIGH LEVEL OF PERSONAL MORALITY?

Recently we have all heard a great number of public voices in the press and electronic media hastening to assure us that it matters not a bit how many mistresses Congressman X has as long as he doesn't put them on the government payroll. The persistence with which this separation of sexual morality and professional ethics is pressed betrays our nation's capitulation to a new set of values in which biological sex is fun and games and need not be an expression of any abiding relationship.

But is it possible to compartmentalize ethical conduct? Extramarital sex involves far more than a physical act. Among other things, it violates a pledge of faithfulness. So the man out on the town who picks up a streetwalker (or, more discreetly, phones for the services of a companion for the evening) is not simply involved in a sexual escapade, he is breaking a contract established by the marriage vow. He is demonstrating an essential lack of basic integrity.

This is why it is of vital importance that men in political office be held accountable, not only for how they spend the taxpayer's money, but also how they handle the taxpayer's confidence. Common sense tells us that if a person will break trust in one area, he may very well break it in some other area. People who cheat on their wives are more apt to cheat on other matters. This is not some sort of domino theory of ethics and morality. It is, rather, a simple observation that if a person allows himself the freedom to follow his desires in one area (sexual promiscuity), he is probably more open to following his desires in another (self-serving legislation).

But, some will argue, isn't a man's personal life his own business? The answer is, No. The foolish idea that anyone can live unto himself alone is romantic fiction. Like it or not, mankind is involved in a web of interpersonal relationships that makes him responsible to all others. If it were true that "every man is an island," then one of the basic elements of humanity would cease to exist. We are what we are in relationship to one another. Without relationship we would not be human. Even the animal world shares a network of instinctual relationships. The goal of "doing one's own thing" is not only sub-human, it is sub-animal. Only vegetables apparently do not enjoy relationships.

It makes a difference if Congressman X adopts a life-style which not only is still unacceptable in general among the constituency but also places him in the position of violating his own sense of what is right and wrong. He has given evidence of a serious character flaw and we may assume that this flaw will affect other actions as well. My position is not one of a dogmatic moralist nor accuser. It is simply the position that flows from the basic premise that moral character cannot be compartmentalized. Man is an entity, a whole, and breach of trust has a debilitating affect on the entire person.

But haven't we had many great leaders in the past who had serious flaws in their personal lives? The answer must be qualified. If by great one means effective, then the answer may be Yes. If by great one means to imply high personal integrity, then I'm not so sure. It would be hard to build a case for the position that if the flaws had not existed they would not have been better leaders. Recognizing that we all fall short of our own ideals (to say nothing of God's) is one thing. But it is quite different to go on to say that therefore ideals don't matter. Even if unattainable, ideals are important. They provide direction towards a way of life which allows us the inner peace that comes from doing what is right. Niebuhr called the ethical code of Jesus "an impossible possibility."

When a person takes public office he assumes certain restraints which are not felt so keenly in the private sector. The ancient Confucian principle that morality should flow downward from the appointed leaders should be sounded anew in the contemporary world. It *does* matter how a person lives: it matters very much how our leaders live.

WHAT DO YOU THINK OF THE MODERN PROTEST MOVEMENTS?

I would say that the right of dissent is a vital and integral part of a free society. The repression of free speech belongs to totalitarianism, not democracy.

This does not imply, however, that dissent has no limitations. Undisciplined "freedom" which rides rough-shod over the rights of others is a negation of the very idea it seeks to establish. Society cannot exist without those restraints which prevent one man from abusing the rights of another. In a mature society such restraints will be to a large degree self-imposed. Where "freedom" has degenerated to a slogan which advocates social irresponsibility, it must be corrected by whatever measures society has developed to protect itself.

YOU NEVER MENTION THE RACIAL PROBLEM. ARE YOU AFRAID TO SPEAK OUT?

The idea that everyone ought to "speak out" on everything is based on the questionable assumption that truth will automatically emerge when everyone starts talking. It is more important for one to have something positive to contribute than it is to maintain a steady flow of verbiage. I do, however, have a few thoughts along the line.

First, the term "racial problem" is a misnomer. Man's one and only problem is sin. Racial prejudice/dislike/fear/etc. is a prominent expression of man's failure to love the Lord his God with all his heart and his neighbor as himself.

Second, it is fair to say that the guilt for social, economic, and political inequality is the guilt of the entire nation. Until man senses his own involvement in the "failure" of others, there is little hope of meaningful progress toward a time when men will do justice, love kindness, and walk humbly with their God (Micah 6:8).

Third, in the new humanity, brought about by Christ's redeeming death, there "cannot be Greek and Jew, circumcised and uncircumcised, barbarian, Scythian, slave, free man, but Christ is all, and in all" (Col. 3:11). Or, as Taylor has it in *Living Letters*, "In this new life one's nationality or race or education or social position is unimportant." Men are men, that's all. All are created in the image of God. All have sinned and "fall short of God's glorious ideal" (Rom. 3:23, *Twentieth Century New Testament*). Whatever differences are discovered and labeled are inconsequential in comparison with their tragic commonality in alienation from God and His divine intention for man.

PSALM 115:16 SAYS, "THE HEAVENS ARE THE LORD'S HEAVENS, BUT THE EARTH HE HAS GIVEN TO THE SONS OF MEN." DOESN'T THIS WARN AGAINST MAN'S EXPLORATION OF SPACE?

One approach to Biblical interpretation encourages the reader to find in ancient Scriptures all sorts of references to technical developments in contemporary life. If that's what the verse means, this questioner certainly has a point! But before we draw what could be a false inference, let's look at the larger context. It is one of the basic rules of interpretation that every statement must be understood over against its own background.

We instinctively recognize this in normal discourse. The statement, "This will kill you" is relatively meaningless until you discover whether the speaker is a mother snatching a bottle of medicine from her child's hand or a good friend about to tell you a funny story. Context is the golden rule of interpretation. Since the

Bible is literature, it must be interpreted by the same general rules as any other book. A single verse means exactly (and only) what it means in its own literary and cultural context.

Picture the Palestinian countryside some three thousand years ago. Place yourself beside the psalmist as he sits at night on the side of a hill gazing in wonder at the starry heavens. To him the heavens are the place of God's abode and the heavenly bodies the handiwork of the sovereign Creator. But, as man, he himself belongs here on the earth. Sensing the majesty and greatness of God, he acknowledges the infinite distance between himself and the Creator by confessing, "The heavens are the Lord's heavens, but the earth he has given to the sons of men."

It would be unfortunate to read into this marvellous expression of reverential awe some mundane instructions about space travel. This sort of hyperliteralism would pervert the intended meaning by the ridiculous method of reducing every expression to its primary (or denotative) dictionary definition.

RECENTLY A FACTORY WORKER IN ILLINOIS WON A STATE LOTTERY OF $300,000. WHAT DO YOU THINK ABOUT THIS KIND OF 'GAMBLING'?

I saw the picture in a local newspaper of the young man who had just won $300,000. He was pictured leaping off the front steps of his house in absolute ecstacy. Hard to argue that he wasn't enjoying his good fortune!

Why should anyone claim that this sort of good luck or reward is in any sense immoral? Isn't it a humane thing to make possible financial security for a factory worker?

The basic question in this consideration is, Who made this "jackpot" possible? Money must come from somewhere.

The money came from other people. People who also bought lottery tickets and waited expectantly for their number to come up. They paid for the good fortune of the winner.

But, weren't they willing to? Didn't they buy their tickets with the realization that their chances of winning were quite slim? Yes, they did. But the lure of getting something for nothing was so strong that they took the chance.

It is here that society needs an adequate view of man's nature. Man has certain tendencies which can be exploited by others. The vision of instant wealth preys upon men and in a moment of weakness they will risk a great deal to make it come true. In the gambling centers of the United States people stand mechanically in front of machines which are pre-set for a certain percentage of return to the house, and what remains is for the player. I am told that currently the house gets about eighty-four percent!

Levers are pulled, and pulled, and pulled. Whenever someone hits a jackpot it is announced over the loudspeaker, and players redouble their determination to go home with a windfall.

Is this sort of thing the basis of a sound society? Are the qualities that make a nation great developed by an appeal to human cupidity? Is it an honorable expectation to get a huge personal reward paid for by others, even if they paid willingly?

But do people gamble of their "own free will"? The compulsive gambler, by definition, is a victim of his own drives and can hardly be said to be *free* to gamble or not. What of others? Here the answer seems to be a matter of degree. Everyone is to some extent "bound" to act for his personal advantage. Although Christians are freed from egocentrism by their union with Christ, the "old man" still struggles to control their actions.

I would think that a sound society based on Christian principles would resist any attempt to provide windfalls for individuals at the expense of others. In the early church those who had lands or houses sold them, laid the proceeds at the apostles' feet "and distribution was made to each as any had need" (Acts 4:34-35). This approach runs exactly counter to the self-serving greed of gambling.

SINCE THE BIBLE SAYS THAT "BODILY EXERCISE PROFITETH LITTLE" (I TIM. 4:8) WHY DO CHRISTIANS GET SO INVOLVED IN SPORTS ACTIVITIES?

"Bodily exercise profiteth little" *appears* to suggest that it is of little use to become involved in any program of regular physical exercise. Jogging, or whatever, is essentially a waste of time. But does Paul *mean* that? A quick survey of several modern speech translations suggests that the apostle is not putting down physical fitness. The RSV says, "Bodily training is of some value," and Williams writes, "Physical training, indeed, is of some service." Who is right? To answer this requires a look at the slightly larger context.

A composite paraphrase of I Tim. 4:7-8 could read as follows: "As for profane legends and old wives' tales, leave them alone (20th Century NT). Spend your time and energy in the exercise of keeping spiritually fit (Living Letters). Bodily fitness has a certain value but spiritual fitness is essential (Phillips) since it carries with it a promise of life, both here and hereafter" (Montgomery). The issue is not whether physical exercise is of value but whether spiritual fitness is of *supreme* value. The argument is that of the lesser to the greater.

If you accept the premise that spiritual fitness is of greater ultimate significance than physical fitness, and in fact you do involve yourself in a program of sorts which leads to a strong and healthy physique, then how much more should you enter into a program of training in godliness which will result in a healthy spiritual condition! Especially since its benefits go beyond this life into the next.

Let me put the issue to you in a different way. Hockey is a tremendously exciting game. From the first faceoff until the final siren it is packed absolutely full of dramatic spinetingling action. It is a game meant only for those willing to give it everything they've got. The goalie is called on to withstand two hundred pounds of coordinated muscle as it bears down with lightning speed to drive the puck toward his goal at speeds in excess of one hundred miles per hour.

Or, let's talk about wrestling. Have you ever watched a good collegiate wrestling match? Have you seen the tremendous exertion of a man who, having lost the advantage, is barely keeping his shoulders off the mat? Here is a sport that calls for strength, balance, timing, coordination and cunning. A good wrestler is the product of countless hours of rigorous training and constant self-discipline. It is a sport only for the man who is prepared to give everything he has for a long time.

Why do I talk about hockey and wrestling in this column? Simply because of the shocking disparity between the determination of the athlete and what often passes for Christian commitment. Should not the disciple of Jesus Christ throw himself into the pursuit for holiness with the same abandon that the young athlete gives himself to physical conditioning? Should not our motivation to serve Christ be as strong as our desire to throw a ball through a basket or to slide down a snowy slope on two sticks of wood?

I'm one hundred percent for athletics. I believe in maintaining the bodies which God has given us in top physical condition. I fully appreciate the value of competition. But I am asking, What's wrong with approaching the Christian life with the same vigorous determination? Paul's favorite metaphors were taken from athletic games and military life. Is he not saying that in the Christian race there is room only for those who joyfully give themselves to life's challenge with all the concentrated effort of an athlete bent hard on winning? "So run that you may obtain [the prize]!" (I Cor. 9:24b).

APPARENTLY, NEW AND BETTER METHODS FOR BEHAVIOR MODIFICATION ARE ON THE HORIZON. WHAT POSITION SHOULD THE CHRISTIAN TAKE ON "COMPULSORY MORALITY" AS PROJECTED BY THE SOCIAL ENGINEERS?

The question of behavior modification is one of serious import. Anyone who has read Orwell's *1984* or Huxley's *Brave New World* has been introduced, even though in fantasy, to the frightening prospect of social control by advanced technology.

It is axiomatic that if society is to continue, it must operate within certain acceptable guidelines. Unrestricted personal conduct leads inevitably to social anarchy. Over the long course of history, certain basic rules and restrictions have developed to insure the precarious balance between social stability and maximum personal freedom.

116

The setting of a highway speed limit is a compromise between what may be the desire of an individual driver and what is certainly the welfare of others who wish to use the same thoroughfare. Not honking in a hospital zone is a "restriction" out of consideration for those who need the benefit of a quiet atmosphere for physical recovery. Thus, all the social rules of life are part of a mechanism to adjust the behavior of the individual for the welfare of society as a whole.

What then is wrong with more effective methods of behavior modification? Michael Knight of the New York Times News Service reported a program carried out at Connecticut's maximum security prison in which pedophiles are, on a voluntary basis, taking a twelve-week therapy course involving small electric shocks applied to the inner thigh whenever a picture of a naked child is flashed upon the screen. When adults are shown, there is no shock. The treatment also includes sessions in which the patients under hypnosis are taught to associate objects they fear (such as height, snakes, etc.) with children and pleasurable thoughts with adults.

Apparently it works. Repeated offenders have been paroled after treatment and so far none has been re-arrested. Roger Wolfe, the psychologist who administers the treatments, says that the immediate effect is unquestionable—"It knocks the [expletive deleted] out of their sexual fantasies." The lasting effects, however, are unclear. Civil liberty groups are alarmed because such programs raise the specter of government thought control. The new methods are quick and inexpensive; and if proven successful would be a powerful weapon, should they fall into the wrong hands to silence political dissent.

Is there any such thing as a *Christian* position on an issue like this? If the principle of social control is accepted, why should anyone—and especially the Christian—object to more efficient methods of achieving the same goal? Obviously, there is no proof text that will settle the problem. That society needs some form of control is perfectly obvious. That restrictions influence behavior cannot be denied. But, does it follow that if a little is good, more is better? Or does increased efficiency in behavior modification add another and fatal variant to the social equation?

The flaw in all utopian programs is that at some point or another they involve the disease itself as a vital ingredient in the cure. Human nature is the problem, yet human beings are called upon to conduct themselves as if they were somehow free of the very malaise they must help to eradicate. The fear of the Civil Liberties Union is legitimate: no one can be trusted with absolute power over the behavior of another. The prospects of abuse are so enormous and the prevailing tendency of man to turn every situation to his own advantage so clearly verified in the historical record, that the relatively inefficient methods of social control are to be preferred to the more sophisticated programs which would allow someone somewhere to decide what is moral and effectively carry it out.

The Christian realizes that this world is but a temporary phase in the divine plan. This alone should make him leery of grandiose plans concocted by the social engineers to create a perfect society in which some human agency decides with awesome finality the appropriate limits of social conduct. The Christian's citizenship is in heaven (Phil. 3:20) and while desiring equality and personal liberty for every man he realizes that the only behavior modification method that is meaningful for eternity is the inner transformation wrought by the Spirit of God.

118

The Current Scene

7

More time is spent reading the newspaper than all other kinds of writing put together. Why? Because people are interested in what is going on right now. The current scene has a fascination all its own.

The questions and answers which follow treat a number of current issues which, during the past few years, have been discussed by Christian people.

It is obvious that such questions call for opinions. They are value-laden inquiries. While each requires accurate information of a descriptive nature, the real issues have to do with aesthetic and moral judgments. I offer my answers as attempts to project in a logical fashion the ethical standards of Scripture onto the issues and practices of contemporary life. God's revelation in Christ Jesus is as always the norm. Whether my understanding of Scripture and its implications for life are accurate and appropriate, each reader will have to decide for himself.

ARE THE YOUNG PEOPLE OF TODAY REALLY ANY DIFFERENT THAN THEIR PARENTS WERE AT THE SAME AGE?

In many ways the young people of every age and culture are essentially the same. Being young means dreaming the impossible dream. The fantasies of youth have the great advantage of not being discouraged by the wisdom of maturity. They are unencumbered by the stern realities of life's limitations. Being young means being plunged from exhilaration to despair and immediately recovering in time for another exciting adventure. Young people everywhere have always shared the common experiences of elation and despondency, as well as many other emotions.

What has changed in our day is not so much the raw material of human existence but rather the environment in which it struggles toward maturity. When those who are now just becoming grandparents were growing up, the war which was to have made the world safe for democracy had already been fought and won. A widely-read theological publication gathered up the expectations of an entire generation and confidently heralded the arrival of the "Christian Century."

History has proven this prognosis wrong. In the tread-mill of world events (which continues to increase its speed), World War I was followed by the Great Depression. Then came World War II, followed by Korea and Indochina.

Everyone born within the last quarter century has grown up under the ominous shadow of an enormous nuclear cloud. I am told that the United States and Russia have stockpiled the equivalent of sixty thousand tons of TNT for every man, woman and child on the face of the earth. Other countries are rushing to join the nuclear club. With every new development of destructive potential the fabric of human existence on planet earth becomes thinner and more liable to dissolution.

In a world marked by insecurity it is only natural for young people to seek security however they can. Some turn to drugs, hoping to capture joy while there is still time. Others turn to religion in order to find a "reason for being" in association with the Jesus People or Hare Krishna. All sense the cosmic strangeness of what is most certainly the apocalypse of human history.

There is yet another factor which has made a major impact upon the young in our day. Today's youth belong to an electronic culture. The average college freshman (one survey indicates) has watched about eighteen thousand hours of TV. All psychologists would agree that this sort of saturation exposure alters not only *what* a person thinks but *how* he thinks as well. The rational and intuitive patterns that stem from over-exposure to the tube must of necessity be different. This is not to decry technological progress or to pronounce TV an instrument of the devil. It is only to lament that the fundamental purpose of the industry is not to raise the level of artistic appreciation on the part of the viewer but to deliver him to the sponsor and his pitch. Programs come and programs go, not on the basis of their educational and aesthetic merit but on the basis of their audience appeal. Ratings are the crucial factor. The significance of TV for contemporary culture is that it has altered the tastes of an entire generation. The young are particularly vulnerable.

The answer to the question, "Are young people today any different than their parents were?" has essentially been, No. However, this must be qualified. The world they have inherited has in fact brought about a decided change. The two major factors are the possibility of ultimate destruction and the pervasive influence of mass media. In both areas Christians have a positive contribution to offer. We can demonstrate to a weary world that it is possible for a community of people to live in love. We can also use our time and energy in such a way as to address the real issues of productive living rather than to squander them in the unreal world of media entertainment.

WHAT ABOUT THE WAY YOUNG PEOPLE DRESS? SHOULD CHRISTIAN PARENTS ALLOW THEIR CHILDREN TO WEAR PATCHED JEANS, TORN SHIRTS, ETC.? SHOULD PARENTS INSIST THAT THEIR SONS HAVE SHORT HAIR?

The basic issue here is the symbolic significance of dress and conduct. It seems clear that the way a Christian appears to the outside world should be consonant with what he believes. Paul said that "women should adorn themselves modestly and sensibly in seemly apparel" (I Tim. 2:9). Why? Because modesty is appropriate for women (and men) who profess Christianity (v. 10). How we dress says something about our approach to life. It has symbolic significance.

Hair length is a particularly sensitive issue in a great number of Christian homes. But before we can see this problem in its proper perspective, some misunderstandings have to be cleared up. First of all, there is nothing intrinsically wrong with long hair—nor is there virtue in baldness. Apart from a specific context, hair is hair, no more and no less. Second, the question is bothersome because it seems to suggest that if your son has short hair he is probably an okay Christian kid. It should be obvious that length of hair is not a valid spiritual indicator.

However, in our contemporary culture, the long hair fashion began as a symbol of a movement which was not morally neutral. In his book *Do It!*, Jerry Rubin wrote, "Young kids identify short hair with authority, discipline, unhappiness, boredom, rigidity, hatred of life—and long hair with letting go. . . . Wherever we go, our hair tells people where we stand on Vietnam, Wallace, campus disruption, dope. We're living TV commercials for the revolution. . . . Long hair is the beginning of our liberation from the sexual oppression that underlies this whole military society."

For Rubin and other activists of the sixties, long hair was a symbol of the rejection of the values of Western society. Long hair became a visible way of saying, "Down with the oppressive limitations of society; up with personal freedom."

So far we've been talking about the extremists of a radical era. But what about the boys in the youth group of the local church? They aren't out to overthrow anything. Long hair is merely the style and they like to be with it. It's the same with patched jeans, torn shirts, shoes with holes, etc.

Let's acknowledge the fact that we all like to stay within shouting distance of the fashion parade. Young people want to be in style for the same reasons that Dad doesn't want to drive an old car (unless, of course, it's a classic). The crucial question is, Just how closely do we want to identify ourselves with a movement which in its extreme embraced a wholesale rejection of traditional values? This is a serious question and one which can be answered only by young people themselves.

If parents make their teenager don a Sunday special sport shirt and a pair of carefully creased slacks they don't get at the problem at all. Forcing a teenager to wear yesterday's styles may make him more appealing in the parents' eyes, but it misses the point. Young people need to understand that a person's dress projects his values and self-image. Clothing is a symbolic way of telling others how we view ourselves and our world. Obviously, there should be no great discrepancy between the language of our dress and what we actually believe. If young people decry hypocrisy, here is one place they can stamp it out. It is a question of propriety: When does "style" say the wrong thing about our love for Jesus Christ?

If a parent is willing to break from the pleasure-oriented society in which he finds himself and use his energies for the kingdom of God, he will have less trouble convincing his child that there are more important goals in life than looking like one's peers. If both parent and child have been touched by the redeeming love of Christ, a satisfactory compromise should not be hard to maintain.

WHAT DO YOU THINK OF THE SO-CALLED JESUS PEOPLE?

Although we no longer hear as much about the Jesus People as we once did, the phenomenon has been so widespread and controversial that it merits continuing discussion.

The question poses a problem because the designation "Jesus people" covers a wide range of groups and individuals all the way from the local youth group to the Christian World Liberation Front. It includes the charismatic Linda Meissner and the Jesus People Army in the Pacific Northwest, the flamboyant Arthur Blessitt of cross-carrying fame, Dr. Jack Sparks (Ph.D., Michigan State) in the Bay area, and the spartan Children of God with communes in Texas and elsewhere. In a *Time* article of summer 1972, even Campus Crusade for Christ was placed under the same umbrella. Therefore, what I have to say should be taken only in a general sense of the movement as a whole.

The movement has much to commend it. It takes Christian discipleship seriously. To the dismay of affluent Christianity it demonstrates a willingness to forsake material values and follow the path of the One who had "nowhere to lay his head." The movement places a high premium on the study of the Scripture. The Children of God carry the Bible in shoulderstrap pouches and learn three hundred verses in the first two months. Members of the Christian Foundation in Saugus, California, read nothing but the Bible. (Leader, Tony Alamo, also reads the newspaper and reports on what biblical prophecies are being fulfilled that day!)

Perhaps one of the most dramatic benefits that comes out of the movement is the large number of young people addicted to drugs who are experiencing immediate cure without withdrawal symptoms. Dr. Hardin B. Jones, professor of physiology and medical physics at the University of California, in his extensive research of drug abuse has interviewed many "Jesus Freaks" who tell of a dramatic release from drug dependency following conversion and a period of extended sleep. He acknowledges that there is no adequate scientific explanation for this phenomenon and calls it the closest thing to a miracle that he, as a scientist, has ever seen.

The movement is not with its weaknesses. Experience oriented, it tends to look down on traditional theologies and the role of rational thought. A testimony in *Maranatha,* a Jesus paper out of Vancouver, reads: "How do I know it works? I know by the only method you can really trust . . . by experience. . . . My beliefs merely left me with a messed up head and nothing inside. . . . Experience is what really counts." Unfortunately, the Jesus people are too often known for what they are against. They tend to be anti-intellectual (they delight in quoting, "Hath not God made foolish the wisdom of this world?"), anticultural (the Bible is seen as exhaustive truth rather than the criterion by which to judge all human attempts to discover truth), and anti-church (Jon Braun describes the Brothers and Sisters as a group of disaffected followers of the "secular church" in need of a haven in which to breathe new vigor into the suffocated life of organized Christianity).

This pessimistic view has its own peculiar dangers. One is that thousands of young people can be permanently scarred spiritually. Gary North, writing in *Christian News* (June 4, 1971), tells of antinomian revivals in history which brought people to the peak of enthusiasm and then failed to follow through. As a result, they and the generations that followed them refused to accept anything further that God had for them. Such "burned-over districts" (the expression is Charles Finney's) become completely unworkable fields for future evangelization.

Perhaps one of the greatest needs of our day is for established churches to extend their ministry to include the Jesus people. Most churches need a burst of new life which the young who have abandoned themselves to Christ can provide, and most of the young need the direction and stability which "straight churches" can provide. Alienation between the two can do nothing but work to the disadvantage of both and in so doing hinder the work of Christ in today's world.

IS THERE ANY DANGER IN THE CURRENT TREND IN GOSPEL MUSIC?

In the contemporary church the guitar has become almost as commonplace as the organ. The more stately hymns of yesteryear have given way to experience-centered ballads projected by means of sophisticated electronic gear.

The current trend is toward a kind of music which, on the basis of its melodic line, rhythmic beat, and harmonic texture, would be as acceptable in a totally secular setting as it is in church. My answer is, Yes, gospel rock, jazz, and pop represent an unfortunate trend.

Music is a powerful force in calling forth from man a wide variety of responses. Great music is the result of a great theme finding an appropriate musical expression. Down through the centuries such glorious truths as the sovereign majesty of God, the redemptive love of Christ, and the unspeakable joy of new life in the Spirit have moved composers to write the kind of music which has appealed to the highest and noblest in man.

On the other hand, much modern music elicits primarily a bodily response. The heavy insistent beat of rock and roll traces its musical lineage back through the music of burlesque to the primitive rites of tribal man. The lush harmonies of many contemporary gospel songs seem to be more appropriate to dancing cheek to cheek than to encouraging us to walk in God's footsteps. The basic complaint is not contemporary music itself but its appropriateness as a musical expression of divine truth.

More simply, if the words of a song say "Christ died for me," the melody, harmony, and rhythm should not say "Come dance with me."

HOW WOULD YOU ANSWER THE ARGUMENT, "CHRISTIANS OUGHT TO ATTEND ALL SORTS OF MOVIES—EVEN SEAMY ONES—SO THEY WILL UNDERSTAND WHAT THE WORLD IS REALLY LIKE"?

This question repeats a rather specious argument that is commonly used whever a person wishes to expand the limits of his personal freedom. The argument is built upon two questionable assumptions. The first is that the world as portrayed in cinema is in fact the real world.

It ought to be perfectly obvious, however, that the characters in a movie are the puppets of the screen-writer, director, and producer. Although they act as if they inhabit the real world, they are no more than the author's vision of reality. It lies in *his* power to project a set of values which, although appearing to meet the test of life, is in reality subjective and personal. By the manipulation of his characters the writer can say any-thing he wishes and make it appear true to life. He can effectively convey the idea that commitment to the wel-fare of others is a noble aspiration or he can promote the cynical view that everyone in power is out for himself and ought to be gunned down. To attend a movie is not necessarily to discover what the world is really like.

The second questionable assumption is that exposure to the seamy side of life helps one understand it. (When expanded, the argument continues that Christians live a sheltered existence and need to be shocked into a reali-zation of the depth and extent of human degradation.) But does it actually follow that to view that which is socially and ethically unacceptable is to understand it better? Does the man who has just seen a cinema in which a dozen people are stabbed, shot, or bludgeoned to death (in slow motion, of course, so the viewer may enter more completely into the experience) understand more accurately the nature of the real world? Is it not possible that overexposure to violence may make him less able to understand the unrestrained effects of hatred in the world?

Or, to carry the argument one step further, if viewing violence helps a person understand it, then why wouldn't an actual experience of violence teach all the more? Certainly a real live assault would be a more complete learning experience than simply seeing one in a movie! No, it should be perfectly obvious that exposure to sin is not the best way to overcome it.

Paul says, "Brothers, keep in mind whatever is true, whatever is just, whatever is pure, whatever is attractive, whatever is high-toned" (Phil. 4:8, Moffatt). And again, "If then you have been raised with Christ, seek the things that are above" (Col. 3:1). These "things above" are contrasted with "things that are on earth"—specifically, "immorality, impurity, passion, evil desire, and covetousness" (vv. 2, 5). To fix one's attention, even for a couple of hours, on the seamy side of life in order to understand the real world, is, however well intentioned, a decision which runs counter to the teaching of Scripture. Like Paul in Romans 1:18-32, most Christians are quite aware of man's depravity. Intimate knowledge of the details of debauchery is not part of the armour of God listed in Ephesians 6:13-17.

IS VIOLENCE ON TV ALL THAT BAD OR IS IT JUST ANOTHER FORM OF COPS AND ROBBERS WHICH WE USED TO PLAY AS KIDS?

After reporting the brutal disfiguration of a young married man waiting at a downtown bus stop with his wife and two infant daughters—he was robbed and then had his eye gouged with the broken end of a soft-drink bottle—Richard Starnes, writing for the Newspaper Enterprise Association, concluded, "America, 1975, is a country drowning in its own blood."

Statistics would support this grim conclusion. Five years ago the National Commission on the Causes and Prevention of Violence warned the nation to mend its "bloody-minded" ways. Since then, however, violent crime has increased more than fifty percent. In the last decade and a half, rape, murder, robbery, and assault with weapons have increased over three hundred percent. Some would argue that Americans are a violent people by nature and what has been true of the past will continue in the future. This argument, however, overlooks the fact that between 1900 and 1960 the rate of violent crime per 100,000 was on the decline.

Another disturbing part of the larger picture is the changing nature of the violence itself. The violence which brought the Commission into being was primarily a calculated violence against the establishment—antiwar protests, political assassinations, anti-civil rights demonstrations. More recently, however, violence has become increasingly mindless and irrational. For example, in Mountainside, New Jersey, a bright and personable fifteen-year old hacked his parents to death with an axe and then took his own life by jumping off a water tower. There was no apparent provocation for these tragic acts other than a reprimand for talking in class.

Why the sudden increase in wanton violence? Dr. Murray Bowen, professor of psychiatry at Georgetown Unviersity, understands it as one result of an increasingly anxiety-ridden society. The higher the level of anxiety, the more immature the behavior of people. Immaturity increases all human problems, including violence.

But why the increased anxiety? We must go back one additional step in our analysis. Causes such as recession-inflation, over-population, and depletion of natural resources have been suggested. While such things sap the inner strength of a society, it is hard to believe that they are sufficient causes to turn a people upon itself in a wild binge of self-destruction. They do not explain the shooting of an elementary teacher in Penns Grove, New Jersey (and the killing of the school principal who came to investigate) in plain view before twenty-five second graders.

Something far more sinister is involved. Could it be the presence of the demonic in a society no longer able to discipline itself into some semblance of civility? Dr. Bowen draws the somber conclusion, "We are well on our way, and nothing is going to turn it around. This society is going down the drain."

Does the Christian have any particular insight into this problem? Paul wrote to Timothy of "terrible times in the last days" when people would be disobedient, without love, without self-control, brutal, treacherous, and rash (II Tim. 3:1-4). In an earlier letter he spoke of "the power of lawlessness" which, although held back for a time, was already at work (II Thess. 2:7). The Christian's insight is that behind the scenes of history there is a struggle going on between the powers of darkness and the God of light. Satan, although defeated on Calvary, is making a final assault. John writes, "He is filled with fury, because he knows that his time is short" (Rev. 12:12).

How does violence on TV relate to this larger picture? It is obvious that children cannot come away from a steady diet of violence on TV without it having a detrimental affect upon their lives. Commercial enterprises invest millions of dollars in advertising on the premise that conduct is altered by exposure to a message. Is the "message" of the program any less effective than the message of the commercial?

In earlier days, the cops and robbers days, the good guys could always be distinguished from the bad guys. More recently, roles have become mixed and violence is liable to be associated with almost anyone. This must inevitably alter the consciousness of youth in their relationships with every sector of society. While violence on TV is not the sole cause of violence in society, it cannot be discounted as an important factor in its alarming rise. In Philippians 4, Paul counsels believers to think about things which are true, noble, right, pure, and lovely—a difficult assignment if we turn our minds over to whatever the entertainment industry, in response to commercial gain, decides to put on the tube.

WHAT DO YOU THINK ABOUT NUDITY ON THE STAGE?

While only a small percentage of Christians across the nation attend the legitimate theatre with any regularity, all have read reports of this modern trend in the entertainment field. In an increasingly permissive society the popularity of plays such as *"Hair"* is to be expected. If the *only* restrictions on conduct are what the public will accept at a given time it seems obvious that before long anything will go. Fortunately, a segment of society—although increasingly small and less vocal—is governed by standards which do not shift with passing fancies. It remains to be seen whether there are enough "salty" Christians to preserve contemporary society (Matt. 5:13).

Paul wrote in rather candid terms when he said of the body that "our unpresentable parts are treated with

132

greater modesty" (I Cor. 12:23). Elsewhere he wrote, "Women should adorn themselves modestly" (I Tim. 2:9). For those who are committed to Scripture as the norm for Christian conduct, this would seem to settle the question of nudity. The argument that nudity is appropriate as an honest art form and that evil is in the eye of the beholder makes good copy but, like all half-truths, misleads by distortion.

HOW DANGEROUS ARE THE DRUGS USED BY MANY YOUNG PEOPLE?

No discussion of the contemporary scene would be complete without some mention of the drug culture.

There are a number of pamphlets available which identify in a rather technical way the difference between the various drugs in use in the counter-culture today. More helpful, perhaps, is a book such as Lewis Yablonsky's *The Hippie Trip* which treats the entire phenomenon of drug use in its larger social context. At one place he writes, "Marijuana is the alcohol of the hippie culture. They use pot like straight society uses alcohol. . . . On the other hand, LSD is the philosophical and religious drug . . . the drug that they use to scramble the circuits, so that they can forget all the social nonsense they were taught by their parents and society." Speed (methedrine and the amphetamines) is in another category. It results not so much in euphoria as an acceleration of the central nervous system (hence the name "speed") providing an intense and compulsive feeling of being "high." According to Yablonsky the use of speed is deplored by high priests of the hippie cult, and even by addicts themselves.

The exact extent of damage caused by drugs is not known. The following observations by qualified researchers, however, should put a large question mark over the entire practice. Dr. Constandinos J. Miras, who has researched for over twenty years the use of marijuana alleges that chronic users are prone to lowered inhibitions, anemia, respiratory problems, and abnormal brainwave readings. Dr. Duke Fisher, who conducts LSD research at UCLA, lists a series of negative results from uncontrolled LSD use, including increased suicidal tendencies, a drastic shift in values, and psychotic behavior patterns. Dr. Samuel Irwin of the University of Oregon in a recent research project found significant chromosome abnormalities among seventy-five percent of the LSD users he tested. The evidence of severe brain damage in speed users has been well established. Although the many users view pot and LSD as aids to a religious experience, the practical results of such mysticism can be seriously questioned. I find myself in agreement with James Denney who said he'd rather be "found in Christ than lost in God."

As an addendum may I register a complaint about the tendency in Christian circles to borrow cult terms from alien ideologies. For instance, the expression *getting high on Jesus* is as misleading as it is distasteful. Where in Scripture can you find anything about denying oneself, taking up the cross and following Christ resulting in some great "high"? It seems to me that cheerful obedience and self-forgetful concern for others is the Christian path. A pathological need for self-centered emotional binges is a sign of spiritual immaturity. If joy and deep satisfaction come in the wake of obedience, so much the better, but such bonuses are neither the purpose of the Christian life nor related to the drug user's "high."

DO THE DAILY HOROSCOPES IN THE NEWS-PAPERS HAVE ANY CONNECTION WITH THE "OBSERVER OF TIMES" IN DEUTERONOMY 18:10, LEVITICUS 19:26, AND II KINGS 21:6?

The expression "observer of times" in Deuteronomy 18:10 (translated "sorcerer" in the RSV) refers to a form of divination in which coming events were extracted from reluctant gods by means of magic and ritual. In Leviticus 19:26 the reference is to witchcraft and is probably connected with the practice of necromancy, or consultation with the dead.

In Deuteronomy 18, the children of Israel were instructed to refrain from adopting the abominable practices of the Canaanites upon entering the promised land. God did not allow His people to resort to divination because He Himself would raise up for them a prophet through whom He would speak (Deut. 18:15-19). Sorcery has no place where God speaks with clarity and finality. Diviners, soothsayers, augurers, sorcerers, charmers, mediums, wizards, and necromancers are an abomination to the Lord (Deut. 18:10-12).

The avid interest in astrology is a contemporary cultural phenomenon of astounding proportions. Writing horoscopes has become big business in our day. This question about reading horoscopes comes up repeatedly in conversations. I would say that the verses in Leviticus and Deuteronomy deal only indirectly with the subject of horoscopes. Of course, for a Christian to regulate his life on the basis of syndicated occultism rather than the Word of God is most certainly ill-advised. It would be parallel to Israelitish idolatry which brought about the divine displeasure of God. On the other hand, astrology in Scripture is not so much condemned as it is belittled.

Isaiah writes with more than a touch of irony, "Stand fast in your enchantments . . . with which you have labored from your youth; perhaps you may be able to succeed. . . . Let [your many counselors] stand forth and save you, those who divide the heavens, who gaze at the stars, who at the new moons predict what shall befall you" (Isa. 47:12-13).

The current surge of interest in horoscopes is a corollary to modern man's faltering confidence in traditional religion. As God is gradually phased out, man—being incurably religious by nature—must find some metaphysical substitute to fill the vacancy. And true to form, superstition is always at hand for this purpose.

IS THE FEMINIST MOVEMENT COMPATIBLE WITH PAUL'S TEACHING ABOUT THE ROLE OF WOMEN IN SOCIETY?

The goal of the feminists is to liberate woman from her historic role of existing for the benefit of man and accepting subjugation and oppression without complaint. (See Susan Brownmiller's article entitled "Sisterhood Is Powerful" in the March 15, 1972 edition of *The New York Times Magazine*.)

Paul seems to have a different opinion about the role of women. They are to adorn themselves modestly (I Tim. 2:9), keep silent in church (I Cor. 14:34-35), and not teach or have authority over men (I Tim. 2:12). It is clear that today's feminists march to the beat of a different drum.

There is little doubt that Paul is *persona non grata* with the modern feminist movement. Was he both a misogynist and a male chauvinist? Are Paul's instructions about women in the church meant for today?

In understanding the problem this question poses, it is well to consider the difference between the basic ethical principle and its application in a particular culture. In the case of women's secondary role in the early church, the principle was not so much the place of women as it was the quality of leadership. In those days women held an inferior status in society at large which deprived them of such advantages as education and leadership training. In view of this situation, Paul would say, the well-being of the church should not be jeopardized by unqualified leadership.

This principle is as true today as it was then. The form in which it is expressed may be considerably different. This is not to say that the goals of the new feminism are compatible with apostolic teaching. Paul distinctly places the husband in the role of responsible leadership, using as his model the fact that Christ is the head of the church. (Eph. 5:22-24).